Medicaid and Long Term Care
in Michigan

Getting Good Care Without Going Broke

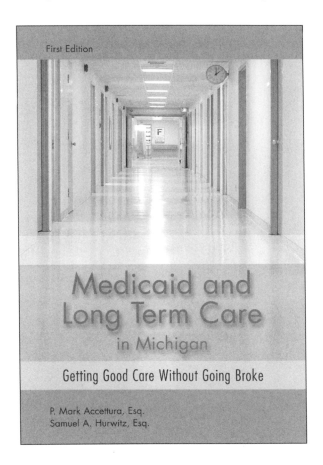

First Edition

Medicaid and
Long Term Care
in Michigan

Getting Good Care Without Going Broke

P. Mark Accettura, Esq.
Samuel A. Hurwitz, Esq.

Medicaid and Long Term Care

in Michigan

Getting Good Care Without Going Broke

Medicaid and Long Term Care

in Michigan

Getting Good Care Without Going Broke

P. Mark Accettura, Esq.

Samuel A. Hurwitz, Esq.

C·O·L·L·I·N·W·O·O·D
P·R·E·S·S

Farmington Hills, Michigan

P. Mark Accettura, Esq.
Samuel A. Hurwitz, Esq.

Collinwood Press, LLC
35055 W. 12 Mile Road, Suite 132
Farmington Hills, MI 48331

The information contained in this book is not intended to be comprehensive and should not be construed by readers as individual legal advice. The laws pertaining to Medicaid and long term care are inherently complex and constantly changing. Any planning strategy must be reviewed in light of current and future law changes. Therefore, readers should consult an experienced elder law attorney for specific legal advice regarding their individual needs.

Cover Design and Page Layout: Deborah Rutti, Network Galleries
deborah@networkgalleries.com

Cover Photo: © www.photos.com

Library of Congress Catalog Number: 2005901858

Printed in the United States

International Standard Book Number: 0-9669278-3-4

TABLE OF CONTENTS

Introduction   1

Acknowlegement   9

Chapter One – Obtaining Authority   11
General Durable Powers of Attorney 12
Medicaid Durable Powers of Attorney 13
Durable Powers for Health Care 14
Do-Not-Resuscitate Order. 17
Guardianship and Conservatorship 17
    Guardianship. 18
    Conservatorship 19
Protective Order. 20

Chapter Two – Selecting Appropriate Long Term Care   23
Independent Living 24
    Retirement Communities 24
    Senior Apartments. 25
    Subsidized Senior Housing. 25
    The Assessment Process. 26
    Home Care: "Aging in Place" 27
    Care Management. 28
Assisted Living Facilities. 29
    Adult Foster Care (AFC) Homes and Homes
      for the Aged (HFAs) 30
    Adult Day Care 31
Nursing Home 32
    Evaluating the facility 32
    Form of Payment. 33
    The Nursing Home Contract 34
Continuing Care Retirement Communities (CCRC). 37
Hospice 39

Chapter Three – Government Funding of Long Term Care   41
Medicare 42

Nursing Home Care. 42
In Home Care 43
Medicaid 44
Nursing Home Care. 44
In home Care 46
MI Choice 46
Miscellaneous Programs. 48
Home Help Program 48
The Michigan Aging Services System (MASS). 48
Program of All-inclusive Care for the Elderly (PACE). 48
Veterans Benefits. 49

Chapter Four – Getting Help   **51**
Area Agency on Aging 51
Ombudsman Program 52
Private Geriatric Case Manager. 53
Hospital Discharge Planner 54
Medicare Medicaid Assistance Program (MMAP) 55
Single Point of Entry 55
Other Resources 56

Chapter Five – Medicare and Medicaid Eligibility   **59**
Medicare 59
Summary of Medicare Skilled Nursing Facility Coverage . . 61
Summary of Medicare In-home Coverage 61
Private Pay 61
Medicaid 61
Eligibility. 62
Income Test. 62
Asset Test. 63
Married Applicant 63
Jointly Held Assets. 63
Snapshot Date 64
Exempt Assets 67
Principal/Residence 67
Income. 68

Patient Pay Amount 68
Spousal Income Allowance 69
Divestment. 70
Look Back for Transfers to Trust 72

Chapter Six – Medicaid Planning Techniques and Strategies   77
Gifting 77
Convert Countable Assets to Exempt Assets. 78
Pay Family Members for Service. 78
Serial Divestment 79
Spousal Annuity Trust 80
Half a Loaf 81
Annuities 82
Retirement Accounts 83
Medicaid Application 84
Annual Reporting. 85
Follow Up for Married Applicants 85
Fact Pattern One 87
Fact Pattern Two 89
Fact Pattern Three 91

Chapter Seven – The Future   93
State Reaction. 93
Estate Recovery 94
Move to More In Home Community Based Care 95
The Nursing Home Industry. 96
Be Proactive 96

Chapter Eight – Long Term Care Insurance   99
What to Look for in a Policy 101
Definitions and Explanations. 103
    Adequate Monthly Benefit. 103
    Benefit Period and Policy Limit 103
    Elimination Period (Waiting Period) 105
    Inflation Protection. 105
    Guaranteed Renewable 106

Waiver of Premium 107
Major Covered Services 107
Tax Qualified 108
Special Tax Situations 110
Self-Employed Taxpayers 110
Corporate Taxpayers 110
Comment 110
Additional Benefits 111
Core Benefit Comparisons 111
The Cost of Waiting 113
Waiver of Elimination Period for Home Health Care 114
Enhanced Return of Premium Feature upon Death 115
Non-Forfeiture Provision 115
Shared Care Rider 116
Family Care Benefits 116
Survivorship and Waiver Benefits 116
Additional Cash Benefits 117
Riders, Riders.....Everywhere 117
Final Note 119

APPENDIX A   **121**
APPENDIX B   **124**
APPENDIX C   **126**
INDEX   **131**

INTRODUCTION

In our collective practice of nearly fifty years, we have watched the aging of our estate planning clients and the evolution of the long term care delivery system. As a natural progression of our practice, we have come to advise our clients on elder law matters including choosing appropriate long term care and obtaining government subsidy for as much of the cost as possible.

We should note up front that we address long term care only as it relates to seniors. We have not attempted to address the long term care needs of handicapped children or other adults.

Unlike the consumers of other products and services, the end user of long term care is frequently *not* the person doing the research. It is often the children of elderly parents who come to us seeking information, and whom we expect will also be the likely readers of this book. Not knowing whether you, the reader, are seeking information for yourself or a loved one, we will simply refer to you, as *you*.

The care options available to seniors who can no longer independently perform all of their activities of daily living (eating, dressing, bathing, etc.) or instrumental activities of daily living (managing money, shopping, taking medications, etc.) are numerous, overlapping, and confusing. Care options range from in-home services for those with modest impairments to nursing home care for those whose function has been significantly affected. In the middle is a broad and growing category called *assisted living* for seniors who can no longer live at home but do not require professional nursing care. Assisted living includes adult day care, adult foster care homes (AFCs), homes for the aged (HFAs), and other group living arrangements that provide supervision, as well as social and recreational activities. Residents of assisted living facilities may also purchase assistance with activities such as meals, laundry and housekeeping if they so elect.

Choosing the appropriate care option begins with an assessment of your needs and functional abilities. Ideally, you would move from independent living in your own home to assisted living and then to a nursing home as your capacity to care for yourself diminished. At each step, you would be evaluated to properly match the level of care to your needs.

In practice, many seniors live in their home beyond the point that they can safely provide for themselves, and then due to a sudden event such as an accident or illness must be moved to an assisted living or nursing home facility. The result is that hasty decisions are often made that overlook various in-home assistance options. Planning in advance will give you the greatest likelihood of obtaining the best possible care, and allow you time to make yourself eligible for the government assistance to which you are entitled. Also, as you will see in Chapter Three, many programs have long waiting lists. Those who start early stand the best chance of securing scarce government services and benefits.

The long term care system in this country is complicated and fragmented. It is *unlikely* that you will be able to obtain the best and most affordable care without help. Fortunately, there's lots of help available if you take the time to look. Help in assessment, care planning, plan implementation, negotiation, monitoring, and advocacy is available through a number of sources including your local Area Agency on Aging (Appendix A), long term care ombudsman (Appendix B), hospital discharge planner, and various private geriatric care managers. Each of these resources is invaluable in helping you sort out your options. Naturally, the more time you have to explore your options the better. You will need time to research your care options, including the individual facilities and service providers. This is especially true if you hope to obtain in-home care that will require you to create a patchwork of in-home care services. Also, it is extremely important that you meet with a qualified elder law attorney as soon as possible to begin the Medicaid qualification process discussed in Chapter Six.

The first step is to ensure that your loved ones have the power to act on your behalf in the event that you become incompetent. Again, our experience has been that very few people make their own long term care arrangements. Whether due to neglect or denial of their failing capacity, the task of arranging for long term care is often thrust upon close family and friends with little or no advance notice. Family and friends often recognize their loss of capacity, and the danger of their living alone, long before they do. Almost universally, it is the family who comes to our office seeking our advice about the senior's options rather than the senior himself. For this reason, we recommend that you grant durable power of attorney to trusted family and friends while you are competent. Trusted family members or friends must have the power to interface with government agencies, home care service providers, and nursing home proprietors. Ironically, seniors often rebuff their loved ones, not wanting to give up control until the absolute last minute, and sadly, often too late. If you do not grant others the power to act on your behalf while you are competent, your family will be forced to obtain guardianship and conservatorship from the probate court in a formal probate proceeding.

Even more confusing than your long term care options are the methods of paying for care. Government assistance for in-home and institutional long term care is available to those who meet stringent medical and financial eligibility tests. Medicaid and Medicare are the two principal government programs that pay for long term care. Basically, *Medicare* pays for in-home and institutional short term care following a hospital stay, while *Medicaid* pays for long term care after Medicare coverage runs out and you have exhausted all but $2,000 of your non-exempt assets.

The key is to get started early. It will take you time to investigate your options, interview service providers, and visit facilities. Also, many of the programs offered by MI Choice (the state run Medicaid program for in-home assistance) have long waiting lists. If your best option is a nursing home, it is important that you enter the nursing home *before* you have spent your assets down to $2,000. If you attempt to enter the nursing home after you have spent down all of your assets, you will have difficulty gaining admission to a suitable facility. On one end of the spectrum are private pay nursing homes – usually the nicest facilities – that do no accept Medicaid patients (which is what you would be with only $2,000 of countable assets). On the other end are nursing homes whose beds are all Medicaid certified, such facilities will likely not offer the quality care you seek. Ideally, you are looking for a facility with a portion, but not all, of its beds Medicaid certified. Such mixed facilities have the ambiance and care of a private pay facility, *and* will allow you to stay after you have spent your assets down to $2,000. A mixed facility will give priority to applicants who demonstrate the ability to private pay for a period of time before becoming eligible for Medicaid. If you wait too long and attempt to enter a mixed facility after your assets have been depleted, you will likely be turned away or placed on an interminable waiting list. The nursing home, faced with its own financial pressures, and the reality that private pay and Medicare reimbursement rates are substantially higher than the Medicaid rate, will hold their Medicaid beds for existing private pay patients. Although discriminating on the basis of ability to pay is against the law, it is a common practice.

Medicaid pays for nursing home care, not assisted living –a concept referred to as Medicaid's *institutional bias*. Be careful that you don't remain in assisted living (or receive expensive in-home care) too long. If you stay until your money runs out, you won't have the private pay funds necessary to enter a nursing home that accepts both private pay and Medicaid patients.

The average monthly cost of nursing home care in Michigan is $5,367 (2005). Without timely planning, your life savings can be quickly exhausted. Health insurance does not pay for long term nursing home care, so it's important to seek and obtain Medicare and Medicaid assistance to defray the cost of long term care. Medicare will pay for the full cost of the first twenty days of nursing home care if it immediately follows and is related to a hospital stay, and a portion of the following eighty days, but it does not address truly long term needs. Without the planning described in Chapter Six, you would be responsible for your own long term care until you had exhausted all but $2,000 of your countable assets. Certain assets, like your house, car, and other items described in Chapter Six are not counted.

As a welfare benefit, Medicaid only provides for basic needs. You or your family must provide for your own personal needs, such as clothing, travel, as well as special medical and dental care. Without planning, you may be left with little or no assets from which to pay the growing number of services and amenities not covered by Medicaid. Other family members may be forced to pay your way or watch as you go without. Fortunately, there are a number of legally proven strategies discussed in Chapter Six that allow you to become Medicaid-eligible without exhausting all of your assets. To employ the Medicaid strategies discussed in Chapter Six you must either be competent, or grant someone authority to act on your behalf in a Medicaid friendly durable power of attorney. Since some of the strategies take several months to employ, it is critical that you execute a Medicaid durable power of attorney in the event you become incompetent during the process.

Many of the Medicaid strategies involve some form of gifting. Michigan law does not recognize the power to make gifts unless the power to gift is specifically referenced in the power. A general power of attorney that is part of a typical estate plan or a power of attorney you get at the hospital or on-line will generally not contain appropriate gifting language. You need the assistance of an elder law attorney to prepare a proper Medicaid durable power of attorney.

People seem very familiar with the rule that you cannot qualify for Medicaid by giving your assets away just before you apply. On the surface, the Medicaid divestment rules do appear to bar the transfer of assets *(for less than fair consideration)* within thirty-six months of your application for Medicaid, or five years for transfers in trust (we often refer to the person applying for Medicaid as the *applicant*). In practice, substantial planning is permitted within the *look back* period (the thirty-six or sixty month period) since transfers made during the look back period cause disqualification for a limited period measured by dividing the amount transferred by the average monthly cost of nursing home care in Michigan $5,367 (2005).

Some have criticized the type of Medicaid planning outlined in Chapter Six as *inheritance protection* and somehow *wrong*. They argue that such planning violates the spirit of the law, creates artificial poverty, and shifts the burden for long term care to the government. We disagree. The law clearly delineates where the government's responsibility ends and where the individual's responsibility begins. As with the income and estate tax laws, we counsel our clients to follow the laws strictly to pay as little tax as possible. In the area of taxation, no one would argue that you should pay any more tax than you are legally required; why should you pay more than your fair share of nursing home costs?

There is a strong sentiment among older Americans that the government should subsidize their long term care. They believe that their life savings shouldn't be wiped out if they require an extended stay in a nursing home. Certainly, the Michigan legislature is well aware of this sentiment, fearing a senior voter backlash if they tighten the Medicaid system to either prevent all forms of divestment or enact estate recovery (discussed later). It is this strong belief that fuels Medicaid planning. No one should underestimate the passionate resolve of most seniors that their nest egg belongs to them and their children and should not be touched by government.

We recommend that you follow the law, but not follow it blindly. Today, ignoring your options can wipe you out financially. If you are married, you must be assured that your *community spouse* (the term used to define the non-institutionalized spouse) has sufficient assets to care for him or herself if you go into the nursing home. If you follow the techniques described in this book, you will preserve you and your spouse's (if applicable) financial security and peace of mind. As our population ages and as federal and state resources become more strained, it will become increasingly important to understand how the long term care delivery system works. Savvy consumers will receive the best available care and the greatest federal and state reimbursement.

If the current state of affairs doesn't sound promising, it's going to get worse. States, with shrinking revenues and an aging citizenry and the federal government with its spiraling deficits have been forced to cut back on their Medicaid budget. As baby boomers begin to age, the pressures on the system will become even more intense, requiring you to become even more savvy in your search for shrinking resources.

Despite the recent national focus on the Social Security system, many believe that a much greater crises looms for Medicare and Medicaid. When it comes to retirement, the American public long ago came to the realization that they cannot count on government alone to provide for their retirement. Interestingly, no similar epiphany has occurred in the area of long term care. We have included a chapter on long term care insurance in the belief that in many cases it is prudent to transfer the risk of an extended nursing home stay to an insurance company. If you are relatively young and healthy, and have disposable income or assets, you should consider purchasing long term care insurance. In addition to traditional nursing home coverage, long term care insurance can be customized to cover forms of care for which little or no government assistance is available: in-home care and assisted living.

The cartoon that follows, and the amusing names used in the examples, portray our attempt to add a little levity to a weighty subject.

"Are you sure this ice floe is going to pass by the nursing home?"

ACKNOWLEDGEMENT

We thank our clients for all that we have learned in the process of helping them. Thank you to Sandra Reminga and the good people at Area Agency on Aging 1-B for their valuable knowledge and input. Thanks to Nida Donar of Citizens for Better Care for her help. Many thanks to Deborah Rutti our graphic artist who always does such a great job (deborah@networkgalleries.com) and to Margie Mackson and Carolyn MacMillan of Senior Solutions of Michigan, L.L.C. (www.seniorsolutionsmi.com); the most caring and professional private geriatric care managers we know. Also, thanks to James M. Knaus, CFP for his contribution of Chapter Eight on Long Term Care Insurance and for the humorous character names used throughout the book.

Notes

Chapter One

Obtaining Authority

It is important that you grant authority to trusted friends and family to act on your behalf in the event you become incompetent. Generally called *advance directives,* such grants of authority take the form of durable powers of attorney and do-not-resuscitate orders. Armed with the authority to make your personal, financial, and health decisions, your chosen advocates, working on your behalf, can access your funds, enter into contracts, apply for government benefits, and appeal the denial of benefits. At a minimum, we recommend that all of our clients create a Will, a general durable power of attorney, a general power of attorney for health care, and a revocable trust (See *The Michigan Estate Planning Guide 2nd Edition,* Collinwood Press 2002). We also recommend a special Medicaid general durable power of attorney where an extended nursing home stay is anticipated.

Absent powers of attorney, your loved ones must obtain authority to act on your behalf by petitioning the probate court for guardianship or conservatorship. As you might expect, obtaining authority from the probate court is much more difficult, time consuming, and expensive than simply signing powers of attorney while you are competent. To make matters worse, your family is put in the awkward position of having to declare you incompetent, an essential prerequisite to any guardianship or conservatorship action.

Timing is extremely important: only a competent individual may execute a power of attorney. Despite our best efforts, there are those who fail to plan for the day when they can no longer care for themselves. Whether due to denial, distrust, or plain old neglect, they simply don't get around to it. In those situations, the family is forced to obtain authority from the probate court.

Whether acting under an advance directive such as a power of attorney, or with the authority of the probate court, your substitute decision maker must act in your best interest. Failure to do so may subject your substitute decision maker to personal liability. On the other hand, since the appointed person is acting in what is called a *fiduciary capacity*, he or she does not become personally liabe under the various agreements executed in his or her appointed capacity. To avoid confusion, agents, guardians and conservators are advised to add words such as "under power of attorney dated _____," or "as guardian," on all contracts and agreements they execute on behalf of the incapacitated person they represent.

General Durable Power of Attorney

A general durable power of attorney allows you, the maker (principal), to appoint another individual (agent) to act on your behalf. As principal, you can delegate to your chosen agent any power you possess personally.

The term *durable* signifies that the power being granted continues to be effective despite the disability of the principal. The term *general* indicates that the power covers a broad spectrum of powers – including banking, preparation and filing of tax returns, and sale of real estate and motor vehicles – permitting the agent to act in your place and stead as if you were present. Depending on the level of trust you have in your agent, your durable power of attorney can be effective either upon execution (signing) or upon your disability (a *springing power*). Naturally, there is a much greater potential for misuse where the durable power of attorney is effective upon signing. For this reason we typically recommend springing durable powers of attorney. However, we recommend that when using Medicaid powers of attorney, discussed below, you grant immediate authority to the agent in order to avoid unnecessary delay in proving your incompetency (which typically requires a doctor's medical opinion).

A durable power of attorney grants to your agent the power to handle all of your *personal* affairs. The power of the agent does *not* typically extend to assets you own in your revocable living trust. Assets owned by your revocable living trust are not considered your personal assets. Your revocable living trust, itself, addresses the issue of your disability through the appointment of a *successor trustee* empowered to act upon your disability.

Under Michigan law, an agent may not make gifts without specific reference to the power to gift in the document. Such power is important in cases where you have commenced an annual gifting program for the purpose of reducing your taxable estate or to engage in the Medicaid planning discussed in Chapter Six. Absent the specific power to gift, your gifting program would be stalled by your disability. In light of the potential for misuse, it is our practice to include only a limited power to gift in our standard general durable power of attorney. A special Medicaid friendly durable power of attorney, with broad gifting powers, should be used where it is anticipated that you may require nursing home care.

Medicaid Durable Power of Attorney

As you will see in Chapter Six, Medicaid planning necessarily involves some form of gifting. Neither Michigan law nor federal law recognizes the agent's power to gift unless it is *expressly* provided for in the document. Thus, special gifting provisions must be added to the general power of attorney of someone who wishes to employ the techniques discussed in Chapter Six.

Similar provisions should also be added to your revocable trust to ensure that Medicaid qualifying gifts can be made by your successor trustee. Your agent (named in your Medicaid power of attorney) should also have the power to revoke, reform, or terminate your trusts as necessary to qualify you for Medicaid.

You cannot assume that an old durable power of attorney drafted as part of your estate plan properly addresses the issues you are about to face. Standard powers of attorney or Designation of Patient Advocate forms are *not* sufficient when it comes to Medicaid planning. A special Medicaid power is required to accomplish the objectives spelled out in Chapter Six.

Naturally, there is great potential for abuse when you grant the power to make gifts to your agent or trustee. For this reason, language limiting your agent's power to self-deal should also be added to your power of attorney and trust. For example, when gifting from the trust, either directly or by creating an interim trust, the agent should be required to *preserve your dispositive scheme* as expressed in your trust document. As a safeguard, your agent may also be required to account to the other family members to minimize suspicions and to maintain open communication with your beneficiaries.

Durable Powers for Health Care

Advances in medical science have created a health care dilemma: how long to keep terminally ill patients alive and on life support systems. Fortunately, Michigan, like all other 49 states, permits the appointment of a substituted decision maker in cases where you are unable to make your own medical decisions. Michigan law recognizes a health care power of attorney, which designates a patient advocate to make your health care decisions including the right to pull the plug in the event of terminal illness. Under Michigan law, the authority of the *patient advocate* comes into effect only when you are unable to participate in your own medical treatment decisions. To preserve your right to self-determination, the law reserves unto you the power to make your own medical decisions as long as you are able. The determination of your ability to participate in medical decisions is to be made by your "attending physician or another physician or licensed psychologist."

Your patient advocate has the legal authority to work directly with your doctors to determine the nature and extent of your medical treatment, including decisions relating to life support system cessation. Absent a properly drafted health care power of attorney, the legal authority to make your medical decisions can only be granted with probate court intervention – by now, everyone is no doubt familiar with the Schiavo tragedy in Florida. In Michigan, living Wills and other informal documents are *not* effective for the purpose of effecting life-ending decisions.

To be effective, a health care power of attorney must be signed in the presence of two witnesses, neither of whom are your spouse, parent, child, grandchild, sibling, heir, physician, patient advocate, or an employee of a life or health insurance provider, health facility, or a home for the aged. The health care power of attorney must be dated, and must contain specific language exonerating health care professionals from liability for terminating life support systems. It must also clearly state that you understand that a decision of your patient advocate "could or would lead to my death." All patient advocates must sign an *Acceptance of Patient Advocate* form, agreeing to act on your behalf in conformity with Michigan law. Perhaps most importantly of all, a health care power of attorney must be signed when you are competent.

Health care powers of attorney should be reviewed and re-executed from time to time. Even valid health care powers can become *stale* if many years have passed since their execution, bringing into question whether they have been revoked or revised in the intervening period. Although there is no time limit on the validity of Michigan health care powers (unlike several other states that limit how many years they are effective), old health care powers of attorney should be replaced every five years or so. Your health care powers should also be reviewed periodically to address changes in the law. For example, we recently changed all of our estate planning documents to address a new health privacy law known as *HIPAA*. The new law affects the disability provisions of all powers of attorney and trusts. HIPAA creates an interesting Catch 22: a doctor's medical opinion is required to activate the disability provisions of your estate planning documents, but the doctor may not discuss your medical status with your family because it violates your privacy! The problem is easily solved by adding a provision to your powers of attorney and trust designating your named fiduciaries as "personal representatives for purposes of the Privacy Rule issued by the U.S. Department of Health and Human Services and required by the Health Insurance Portability and Accountability Act of 1996 ("HIPAA") 45 C.F.R. Parts 160 and 164."

Since it is impossible to address every medical contingency in a health care power of attorney, health care powers tend to grant the patient advocate wide discretion. It is therefore important to choose a patient advocate who understands your wishes, especially with respect to continued life support. For this reason, spouses, parents and adult children with whom you have a trusting relationship are the most logical choices to act as patient advocate. We recommend empowering only one patient advocate at a time. Although it is prudent to name successor patient advocates in the event that your first choice is unable or unwilling to act, naming multiple patient advocates with concurrent powers only creates the possibility for conflict. Hospitals cannot be expected to terminate life support systems when they receive conflicting instructions.

Recent studies have confirmed what the general public had long suspected. Health care directives, even when in writing and communicated to the physician, are frequently ignored by hospitals. For this reason, you must be diligent in implementing your health care power of attorney. The treating physician, hospital, and nursing home should be given a copy of the document. Knowing of the reluctance of hospitals and physicians to remove patients from life support systems, you or your patient advocate must be both assertive and vigilant. It's your right! It is also advisable to verbally communicate your thoughts and wishes concerning terminal illness and life support systems to your patient advocate as well as other family members.

The Patient Self Determination Act requires all Medicare and Medicaid certified hospitals, nursing homes, home health agencies, HMOs, and hospices to inform patients of their right to accept or reject medical treatment and their right to create advance directives such as health care durable powers of attorney. Note, however, that there is no federal law dealing with durable powers of attorney, so health care powers of attorney executed in one state are not necessarily effective in other states. Accordingly, if you split time between or among states you should execute separate health care powers of attorney for each state.

A durable power of attorney may be revoked as long as you are competent. The best way to revoke a durable power is to destroy all copies of the document.

Do-Not-Resuscitate Order

A Do-Not-Resuscitate Order protects terminally ill *home bound* patients by directing that you not be resuscitated in the event your heart stops or you stop breathing. Although Do-Not-Resuscitate Orders do not apply to nursing homes and hospitals, your durable power of attorney for health care can be used to accomplish the same result. See sample Do-Not-Resuscitate Order at the end of this Chapter One.

Guardians and Conservators

Guardians and conservators are court-appointed fiduciaries who represent the interests of incompetent individuals who lack advance directives such as powers of attorney. Basically, a guardian has authority over your person and a conservator has authority over your property. You must be adjudged incompetent before a guardian or conservator can be appointed.

Guardianship

In the event you did not create powers of attorney while competent, authority to act on your behalf must be obtained from the *probate* court, the court with *jurisdiction* in such matters. To have a guardian appointed, it must be shown by *clear and convincing evidence* that you lack sufficient understanding or capacity to make or communicate informed decisions. Additionally, it must be shown that the guardianship is necessary to provide for your continuing care and supervision. This second requirement is intended to uphold the basic philosophy of our legal system: preservation of an individual's right to self-determination. If an alternative to the guardianship is available – such as an existing power of attorney or a do-not-resuscitate declaration – it is generally the view of the courts that the guardianship should not be granted.

The first step in obtaining guardianship is to file a petition with the probate court. The petition is filed by the *petitioner* – who can be anyone interested in your welfare – and is often accompanied by a treating physician's written statement of your medical condition. When granting guardianship, priority is given to your family in the following order: spouse, adult children, and parents. Before granting the guardianship, however, the court must independently verify that your physical and mental condition as represented in the petition is accurate. As part of its investigation, the court will appoint a *guardian ad litem* "GAL" (typically a practicing attorney) to interview you, the petitioner, and other family members, and file a report with the court stating its findings. As further protection, all interested parties (basically your immediate family) receive notice of the proceedings, and are offered an opportunity to object. If the GAL's report supports the appointment of a guardian, and there are no objections from other family members, the court will issue letters of authority granting the guardianship and outlining the powers granted.

Once appointed, the guardian's responsibility is to procure medical and custodial care for you and attempt to restore you *to the best possible state of mental and physical well-being* so that you can return to self-reliance as soon as possible. In making these decisions, the guardian must consult with you if you are lucid and able to communicate. The guardian has the power to consent to or refuse medical treatment. Where no conservator (see below) has been appointed, the guardian must conserve your assets and apply them toward your support and care. The guardian must file an annual report with the court. Note that a nursing home may not compel you to obtain guardianship as a condition of providing care.

Conservatorship

The procedure for establishing a conservatorship is much the same as the procedure for establishing guardianship except that a conservator must procure a bond to protect the assets over which he has authority. To have a conservator appointed, it must be shown by a *preponderance of the evidence* (a lower standard than for guardianship) that you are unable to manage your property and business affairs effectively, and that your assets will be wasted or dissipated unless proper management is provided. The conservator is charged with managing your financial affairs and must file an annual accounting with the probate court. A conservatorship is appropriate when you have substantial assets, and the court determines that protection over and above that available through a guardianship is required. The same person may act as your guardian and conservator. With the court's approval, guardians and conservators may be compensated for their services.

Beyond the expense and emotional toll of going to court, obtaining court authority may take weeks if not months. Although in a true emergency (which is rare) it may be possible to obtain court authority immediately upon the filing of a petition, usual court processes take several weeks to several months to complete, delaying important services and care.

Protective Order

A Protective Order (obtained by petition to the probate court) is appropriate when protection is needed for a particular transaction – as opposed to the ongoing protection of a conservatorship. For example, a protective order might be used when you are about to receive a personal injury settlement that would disqualify you from Supplemental Security Income (SSI). In that case, a protective order may be granted by the probate court allowing your family to establish a special needs trust which would allow you access to the settlement without disqualifying you from SSI.

DO-NOT-RESUSCITIATE ORDER

I have discussed my health status with my physician, _____. I request that in the event my heart and breathing should stop, no person shall attempt to resuscitate me.

This order is effective until it is revoked by me.

Being of sound mind, I voluntarily execute this order, and I understand its full importance.

_____   _____
(Declarant's signature)   (Date)

_____
(Type or print declarant's full name)

_____   _____
(Signature of person who signed for   (Date)
declarant, if applicable

_____
(Type or print full name)

_____   _____
(Physician's signature)   (Date)

_____
(Type or print physician's full name)

ATTESTATION OF WITNESSES

The individual who has executed this Order appears to be of sound mind, an under no duress, fraud, or undue influence. Upon executing this Order, the individual has (has not) received an identification bracelet.

_____   _____
(Witness signature) (Date)   (Witness signature) (Date)

_____   _____
(Type or print witness name)   (Type or print witness name)

THIS FORM WAS PREPARED PURSUANT TO, AND IS IN COMPLIANCE WITH, THE MICHIGAN DO-NOT-RESUSCITATE PROCEDURE ACT

Notes

Chapter Two

Selecting Appropriate Long Term Care

Long term care includes a wide spectrum of services beginning with help with activities of daily living (called ADLs) such as bathing, grooming and dressing, all the way to skilled nursing home care. Long term care can be delivered in a wide range of settings from your own home to a traditional nursing home. The cost of long term care varies depending on the level of care and where it is delivered.

Even today, people who need long term care rely almost exclusively on care provided by family and friends in their own home. Nearly 80% of adults receiving long term care at home rely exclusively on unpaid help. When families cannot do the whole job, because continuous or intensive care is needed, or because caring has become too physically taxing, families turn to more formal arrangements for that care. This Chapter Two will help you identify the long term care options available to you, how to locate them in your area, and what government programs are available to help you pay for the care you choose. We also identify related Web sites and organizations that will help you understand and navigate the long term care delivery system.

It is well established that seniors prefer to remain in their own homes and communities as they age. In recent years, services and facilities have evolved to allow seniors to *age in place*. As you age and begin to require assistance with the activities of daily living, you will need to begin to examine your housing and long term care options. Initially, you may require only supplemental in-home health care and assistance with limited daily activities. The time may come, however, when you will require more intensive care and cannot live alone.

To accommodate the increasing demand for organized housing, a variety of options has sprung up in recent years which break down to three broad categories: independent living, assisted living, and nursing homes. The categories differ primarily in the amount of assistance and care they provide for residents. All three types can be combined in a fourth option – continuing care retirement communities (CCRCs). The discussion that follows takes you through your options starting with the least intrusive and ending with nursing home care. The following is a summary of your long term care options:

Independent Living	Assisted Living	Nursing Homes
• Retirement communities	• Assisted living	• Licensed nursing homes
• Senior apartments	• Licensed homes for the aged (HFA)	• Hospice
• Subsidized Senior Housing	• Licensed Adult Foster Care (AFC)	
	• Home care	
	• Adult Day Care	

Independent Living

Independent living includes senior apartments and retirement communities targeted to active seniors who are able to care for themselves independently. Some independent living facilities offer limited assistance with ADLs.

Retirement Communities

Retirement communities are designed for independent seniors. Sometimes called congregate living, they offer an apartment-like setting with 24-hour on-site supervision.

Services usually include meals, housekeeping and laundry. Numerous social activities help to keep the residents active and foster a sense of community. Only private pay is accepted; no government subsidy is available.

Senior Apartments

Senior apartments allow independent seniors – many of whom may even drive – to enjoy an active lifestyle among their peer group. Senior apartments offer amenities found in other rental communities such as a clubhouse, pool, tennis courts and even golf courses. Although senior apartments typically do not offer 24-hour on-site supervision, they do offer laundry facilities, access to meals, and local transportation on a fee basis. Only private pay is accepted; no government subsidy is available.

Subsidized Senior Housing

The federal government and most states subsidize housing costs for seniors with low or moderate incomes. To be eligible, your adjusted gross income (including interest and dividend income calculated at two percent of the value of your assets) must not exceed $39,150 (2005). Rent is 30% of your adjusted gross income (further reduced by your out-of-pocket medical costs including Medicare and medigap insurance premiums). Although there are no minimum health requirements, you should be able to live on your own without assistance or arrange for your own private-pay on-site assistance. Due to high demand and limited funding, most facilities tend to have lengthy waiting lists: two-years is not uncommon. Facilities usually have on-site do-it-yourself laundry, and occasional meals are available for a token fee. For more information, call the HUD housing counseling locator at 1-800-569-4287, or visit www.hud.gov/local/index.cfm. Application should be made in person at the subsidized senior housing location in which you wish to reside.

The Assessment Process

Assessing your ability to perform *activities of daily living* (ADLs) and *instrumental activities of daily living* (IADLs) is key to selecting appropriate long term care and applying for benefits. ADLs include daily activities such as walking, toileting, continence, eating, bathing, dressing and transferring. You are graded in each activity using the following characterizations: independent, supervision, limited assistance, extensive assistance, and total dependence. IADLs are higher function tasks necessary to live independently such as managing money, shopping, cooking, cleaning, and taking medications. As with ADLs, you are graded on your ability to complete each function. ADL and IADL scores are used by clinicians to develop care plans and by insurers to determine eligibility for benefits and suitability for placement in the appropriate facility. For example, if you can independently perform all ADLs and IADLs, you would not be eligible for many of the programs described in this Chapter Two that require a higher level of functional need. Individuals with IADL difficulties who can perform ADLs independently would not qualify for third party or Medicaid and Medicare assistance, and instead would have to rely on family and community intervention.

Activities of Daily Living (ADL)	Instrumental Activities of Daily Living (IADL)	Range of Ability (from highest to lowest)
Eating	Money Management	Independent
Toileting	Shopping	Supervision
Continence	Meal Preparation	Limited Assistance
Bathing	Housekeeping	Extensive Assistance
Walking	Taking Medications	Total Dependence
Dressing		
Transferring		

Nursing homes evaluate your level of competence in each ADL and IADL and enter their findings on a form called a *Minimum Data Set* (MDS). The MDS report is used by the nursing home for

Medicare reimbursement purposes as well as to establish a *care plan*. The care plan outlines the recommended therapies and nutrition to allow you to attain the highest level of functioning in light of your disabilities. Care plans are revised monthly (or quarterly after Medicare has been exhausted) based on your progress. The more family involvement (and perhaps the advocacy of a private geriatric care manager) in the initial and periodic assessment process the better. No one knows you better than your own family and loved ones, and no one can better protect your interests.

Home Care: Aging in Place

Historically, the bulk of long-term spending has been concentrated on *institutional care;* a phenomenon sometimes referred to as institutional bias. According to AARP, roughly two-thirds (67%) of Medicaid long term care funds go toward institutional care, despite the fact that consumers prefer to remain in their own homes and communities. Perhaps as a reflection of the wishes of our senior population, or because states are learning that home care is more cost effective than institutional care, spending on community based care has been increasing over the last twenty years as more people with long term care needs receive home and community based services. Spending on home and community based services has grown from $1.2 billion in 1990 to $16.4 billion in 2002, representing an average annual increase of almost 25% per year over the twelve-year period. And, spending on home and community based care is accelerating, increasing 83% between 1998 and 2003 alone.

Increasingly, older Americans are choosing to live independently, taking advantage of home care services. This process has come to be known as *aging in place.* The following categories of service, in combination, make in-home care possible:

- *Home care* includes checking blood pressure, monitoring vital signs (blood pressure, blood sugar, temperature) administering medications, changing dressings, and giving injections. Home care services can be provided by traveling physicians, dentists, podiatrists, wound care specialists, licensed nurses and therapists;

- *Personal care* services include help with activities of daily living provided by nurse aides or non-professionals;
- *Custodial care* includes assistance with IADLs like shopping, laundry and meals;
- *Respite care* is 24-hour care either in the home or at a facility that allows family members an opportunity to vacation or just take a break from the care of a loved one; and
- *Adult day care* is daytime care outside the home that allows family members to continue to hold jobs and take a break from the needs of the home care loved one.

If you need extensive daily care at home, you will probably have to pay for much of it yourself. With certain exceptions, government and insurance programs limit home care coverage to specified services on a part-time basis. Medicare and Medicaid will pay for in-home care if you pass the medical and financial eligibility requirements described below. Services such as meals-on-wheels, homemaker services, respite care, and care management, that are funded under the Older Americans and Older Michiganians Acts and administered by local organizations under contract with local Area Agencies on Aging, are more widely available but limited due to low funding. Most Older Americans and Older Michiganians Act services are free, but donations are requested and some services may have a fee schedule based on ability to pay.

Care Management

The number of support organizations and providers of home care is dizzying. Your local Area Agency on Aging, senior center, visiting nurse association, hospice program, hospital, and county health department are all there to help. They, in turn, hook you up with other service providers and agencies, all with their own unique eligibility requirements, pricing structures and funding sources. The problem is compounded when multiple services are needed. Fortunately, relief is available in the form of *care management*. Care management is a planning service, available through your local Area Agency on Aging or from a private geriatric care manager to help you identify and arrange needed long term care services. Care management starts with a thorough assessment of your needs. A care plan is developed from the assessment. Then, using their professional background and knowledge of the long term care delivery system, the care manager implements the care plan by arranging needed services. The care plan and services are reviewed and revised periodically as appropriate.

Assisted Living Facilities

Assisted Living is the fastest growing type of senior housing, providing a combination of housing, support services and health care designed for the individual needs of its residents. Currently, there are no accreditation standards for assisted living facilities in Michigan. Assisted living has become a marketing term that refers to a group living arrangement with private or shared rooms for seniors who can no longer live alone, yet do not need professional nursing care. They offer protective oversight, social and recreational activities, and assistance with activities of daily living. Assisted living communities can be free standing or part of a continuing care retirement community. Licensed adult foster care homes and homes for the aged are also considered forms of assisted living.

Assisted living is significantly less expensive than nursing home care, but is not covered by Medicare or Medicaid. The cost of assisted living varies widely depending on the size of your living area and the services you require. The typical cost of an assisted living facility ranges from $1,500 to $4,000 per month.

Services among assisted living facilities vary greatly, so make sure that the facility you choose meets your needs. The admission contract should be consistent with the facility's stated aging in place philosophy. As you evaluate an assisted living facility, consider whether the facility is willing and able to adapt to your changing needs. Read the admission agreement/contract carefully and make sure that it correctly reflects your understanding of the costs, the services to be provided, and the reasons for being asked to leave. Pay special attention to the reasons for discharge; can you stay if you are incontinent or in a wheelchair?

The Assisted Living Federation of America (ALFA) provides an on-line directory of assisted living facilities and tips for consumers on what to look for when choosing a facility: www.alfa.org (Select "Consumers"). Also see www.michigan.gov/ltc for more information on all forms of long term care.

Adult Foster Care (AFC) Homes and Homes for the Aged (HFAs)

AFC homes and HFAs are long term care facilities licensed by the state. AFCs and HFAs provide room and board, supervision, and ADL services to residents who do not need continuous nursing care. The range of services offered by AFC and HFAs varies substantially, so it is important that the facility you choose matches your needs. HFAs tend to be larger facilities and are often part of a continuing care retirement community (CCRC). AFCs tend to be small facilities (from one to 20 residents) operated out of residential homes (often housing the home's operator). Many AFC homes are dedicated to the developmentally disabled. As they do not provide skilled nursing care, Medicaid and Medicare tend to not cover AFC and HFAs. Whatever government assistance is available is likely to be very limited and subject to long waiting lists. Some help may be available from the Social Security Administration or the Department of Veterans Affairs.

There are over 4,700 adult foster care homes, and about 150 homes for the aged in Michigan. Be on the alert for unlicensed AFC and HFA facilities. Although unlicensed facilities aren't necessarily bad, you do lose the benefit of state inspections and quality control. Additionally, your only recourse against violations of your agreement in an unlicensed facility are the courts, whereas in a licensed facility your state ombudsman will advocate for you.

As with any facility, it is important to review your written agreement, especially with respect to the provisions relating to discharge. You don't want to be forced to leave the facility if your needs exceed the services provided.

You can call the Michigan Department of Consumer and Industry Services for more information about homes for the aged (517) 334-8404, and adult foster care homes (517) 373-8580, or visit the Department of Human Services (DHS) Web site www.michigan.gov/fia. Information about AFCs and HFAs is also available from your local long term care ombudsman (see Chapter Four).

Adult Day Care

Adult day care, when coupled with the traditional family support, has allowed a growing number of seniors to reside in their own home well beyond the point that they can care for themselves. Adult day care, where appropriate, is an extremely cost efficient method of caring for seniors who are unable to care for themselves but who do not require around the clock nursing home care. Adult day care provides needed respite for family members who are employed or otherwise need a break from the duties of caring for their dependent spouse or parent. Naturally, if you are bedridden, or do not have the stamina to function throughout the day, you are not a good candidate for adult day care. Adult day care allows for increased social contact in a supervised setting and includes a range of services including assistance with personal care and activities of daily living. A physician's recommendation is required and applicants are screened to ensure that their needs do not exceed the services available. Other than Medicaid's PACE program, neither Medicare nor Medicaid pays for adult day care.

The Program of All-inclusive Care for the Elderly (PACE), described in Chapter Three, is a federally funded adult day care program. Further information about adult day care can be obtained through the National Adult Day Services Association, c/o The National Counsel on the Aging, Inc. 409 Third Street, SW Washington, DC 20024 (202) 479-1200, Fax: (202) 479-0735, Website: www.ncoa.org

Nursing Homes

The time may come when you cannot properly be cared for in your own home or an assisted living facility and will need the type of 24-hour skilled care only offered in a nursing home. Or, once your money runs out, you may find that as a result of Medicaid's current institutional bias that government assistance is available to you only if you enter a nursing home. Choosing the right nursing home is critical. Not all nursing homes accept Medicaid, and those that do may have only a limited number of beds allocated to Medicaid patients.

Nursing homes provide a wide range of personal care and health services. For most people, the care generally is custodial, or basic in nature including room and board, personal care, protection supervision and medical care. Nursing home residents typically have severe physical or cognitive impairments: they tend to be over age 80, female, without a spouse in the community.

To be admitted to a Michigan nursing home, you must have a referral and recommendation from a licensed physician. To qualify for Medicaid, you must also pass the new medical eligibility requirements discussed in Chapter Three.

Evaluating the facility

A tremendous amount of information is available to help you evaluate nursing homes. State surveyors make unannounced visits to nursing homes every 9 to 15 months to review charts, observe the care being given, and to check sanitary conditions.

Their reports (known as *state survey reports* or *Form 2567*) list each nursing home's deficiencies, and are available to the public. *Consumes Reports* in their *Complete Guide to Health Services for Seniors (2000)* calls the state survey reports "the best piece of consumer information that exists anywhere for any product or service." State survey reports must be posted in each nursing home in a conspicuous place. You can find the surveys on the Nursing Home Compare database on the Health Care Financing Administration's (HCFA) website: www.Medicare.gov. Michigan ranks very high (in recent years, first) in the country in assessing nursing home deficiencies, so if the facility you are investigating has relatively few violations you can be sure that it is a good facility. The state ombudsman (see Chapter Four) also provides valuable information as to the safety and quality of Michigan nursing homes and can recommend nursing homes in your area.

When choosing a nursing home, there is no substitute for visiting the facility and quite literally "sniffing around." Call your local ombudsman and have them give you the names of three nursing homes in your area. Location is important. You want a nursing home close to family so that they can monitor your care and stay involved. Visit the recommended homes and talk to the staff, watch the staff interact with each other and the residents, and talk to other families visiting their loved ones. A complete checklist of things to look for when visiting a nursing home is included as Appendix C and may be useful in your investigation.

Form of Payment

All nursing homes accept private payment and Medicare, but not all accept Medicaid. Those that accept Medicaid may limit the number of beds in their facilities which are certified as Medicaid beds. Some of the higher end nursing homes are private pay only (accepting Medicare for residents who have come from the hospital), and do not accept Medicaid. You would be asked to leave a private pay nursing home once your Medicare benefits (up to 100 days) and money ran out. If you have limited assets and income, or if you intend to employ the Medicaid eligibility techniques described in Chapter Six, you should choose a facility that accepts both private pay and Medicaid patients. The key is to enter the facility as a private pay resident and then convert to Medicaid after you have spent down your assets.

Government programs recognize two types of nursing home care: basic and skilled.

- **Basic Care** – Required to maintain activities of daily living, ambulation, medication management, supervision and safety.
- **Skilled Care** – Requires the services of a registered nurse, on a regular basis, for treatments and procedures.

Most nursing homes offer both skilled and basic care. Medicaid pays for both kinds of care, but Medicare pays only for skilled care. Medicare pays for skilled nursing facility care for a limited period of time if you meet certain conditions described in Chapters Three and Five.

For more information, see *Medicare Coverage of Skilled Nursing Facility Care* (CMS Pub. No. 10153), or contact MMAP (see Chapter Four).

The Nursing Home Contract

Despite the fact that nursing homes may not discriminate on the basis of health needs or financial status, they often do. Nursing homes are motivated by the fact that they are compensated at a substantially higher rate for private pay and Medicare patients than for Medicaid patients. They often practice a subtle form of discrimination in the admission process by requesting detailed income and asset information. From the information you supply, they can determine how long you can afford to private pay before applying for Medicaid. Although this practice is technically prohibited, it is commonplace. If you refuse to provide the requested information, you will typically not be rejected, but will be placed on an interminable "waiting list." If you have minimal or no countable assets, and thus are a Medicaid patient on the day of your admission, you are likely to have difficulty finding a Medicaid bed. You will be told that there is a waiting list for the limited number of Medicaid beds in their facility. Although true, the reason for the waiting list is that the beds are being held for their private pay patients who will convert to Medicaid. Nursing homes will often keep a bed empty waiting for a private pay patient to come along rather than give it to a new applicant with no countable assets. The simple reality is that private pay residents are more profitable to nursing homes and consequently are usually given admission preference. If you are able to find a Medicaid bed as a day one Medicaid patient, it may not be in a facility of your liking. Medicaid facilities simply do not have the revenue to hire the best staff and maintain the best facilities.

Technically, you cannot be asked to private pay for a pre-agreed period of time before applying for Medicaid, nor can homes require a third party guarantee of payment as a condition of admission. The nursing home cannot require a security deposit or other form of pre-admission payment if your care is covered by Medicare or Medicaid. Unfortunately, such practices persist, as laws against such discrimination are not well enforced. If you are signing a nursing home contract as an agent under a power of attorney or as a conservator, be sure to clearly indicate that fact by using words such as "under power of attorney dated _____" to avoid any appearance that you are personally liable under the contract. Although it is extremely unlikely that such a contract would be enforceable against you as a third party, it is best to avoid any potential legal conflict with the facility. Surely caring for your loved one is enough of a undertaking without having to extricate yourself from a sticky legal situation.

Medicaid, the largest payer for nursing home care, has the lowest payment rates:

	Nursing Home Care
Medicaid Reimbursement per day (2005)	$116
Medicare Reimbursement per day (2005)	$268
Average Private Pay Rate per day (2005)	$200*

This figure is based on our informal survey of Michigan private geriatric care managers and differs somewhat from the state's posted daily rate of $177.

Once admitted, you may be evicted only for the following reasons: nonpayment; for medical reasons (you need more or less care than the home can provide); for the physical safety of the staff or the other residents; or because the home closes. You may not be evicted if the assets you disclosed upon admission have been depleted faster than anticipated as a result of employment of the techniques described in Chapter Six.

As with any contract, nursing home contracts should be carefully reviewed to ensure that they are consistent with your understanding of the services to be provided and the costs for those services. You may wish to use the following checklist provided courtesy of Citizens for Better Care in its 1998 publication *The Michigan Long Term Companion.*

Items to be included in the contract:
☐ Services included in daily rate
☐ Services that have an extra charge
☐ Source of payment, such as Medicare or Medicaid
☐ Cost to the resident
☐ Terms of the security deposit, if any
☐ Resident's rights and grievance procedure
☐ Additional provisions agreed to by both parties
☐ Designation of patient representative, if desired by resident

At the signing, make sure you have:
- ☐ A receipt for money deposited in the resident's trust fund, if any
- ☐ A receipt for the security deposit, if any
- ☐ A receipt for any advance payment
- ☐ A copy of the home's residents' rights policy and grievance procedure
- ☐ A copy of the home's policy on advance directives
- ☐ A copy of the signed contract and all attached forms; make sure your copy includes all changes and that they have been initialed by you and the nursing home representative

Make sure that the nursing home has attached to the contract:
- ☐ A signed inventory of the resident's clothing and personal belongings
- ☐ A copy of the patient representative form, if approved
- ☐ A copy of any additional agreements you have made with the home
- ☐ A copy of every other document you sign at admission

Continuing Care Retirement Communities (CCRCs)

Continuing care retirement communities (CCRCs) are residential campuses that provide a continuum of care all in one location. Residents, who must meet financial and health requirements, move from private units to assisted living and then skilled nursing care as they age and require more assistance. Individual condominiums or apartments are available for residents who are still able to live independently; assisted living facilities for residents who need help with daily care; and a nursing home for those who require basic or skilled nursing home care. The principal benefit of CCRCs is that you are guaranteed a lifelong residence, permanently avoiding the emotional and physical stress of moving. CCRCs allow a married couple to live in close proximity where one spouse requires a higher level of care than the other.

CCRCs tend to be high-end facilities for healthy people. They tend to charge a large entry fee as well as an ongoing monthly fee. Some offer the purchase of a condominium or cooperative unit in lieu of the entrance fee. In 2001, entry fees nationally ranged from $60,000 to $400,000 (depending on the type and size on your residential unit), with monthly fees ranging from $700 to $2,500 (depending on the services required). Most entry fees are refundable at death but do not accrue interest during the period held by the CCRC.

Many of the questions that you might ask when investigating a nursing home apply to a CCRC. Information about the CCRC's nursing home should also be available from your local Area Agency on Aging or ombudsman. No federal law specifically regulates CCRCs, but Michigan's Living Care Disclosure Act regulates the terms of their contracts, cancellation of memberships, and membership refunds. Nursing homes within a CCRC are subject to the same state and federal laws that govern freestanding nursing homes. (Because it is a private pay nursing home facility, you may not be able to employ some of the Medicaid planning techniques described in Chapter Six).

You must take into consideration the financial risks of choosing a CCRC. What happens if you don't like the facility, your children move to a different city, the facility goes bankrupt, or the facility declines and you no longer want to live there? The contract terms among CCRCs vary widely, so it is extremely important that you read the agreement carefully – perhaps retaining the services of a qualified elder law attorney familiar with CCRCs.

You can get more information about CCRC from the Office of Financial and Insurance Services at (877) 999-6442, or email your questions to ofis-sec-info@michigan.gov. Also see www.retirementliving.com/michigan.html for information about CCRCs in Michigan.

Hospice

Hospice is special care designed to provide compassion and support for individuals in the final phase of a terminal illness. Hospice care seeks to enable patients to spend their last days with dignity and comfort, and as pain-free as possible. Hospice care can be delivered in a number of settings: in the privacy of your home, in a hospice facility or in a nursing home. To locate hospice services in your area see the Michigan Hospice and Palliative Care Organization Web site: www.mihospice.org/map.vml, or the National Hospice and Palliative Care Organization (NHPC) Web site: www.hospiceinfo.org. The vast majority of hospices are certified to participate in Medicare. Medicare Part A, private insurance and Medicaid all cover hospice. See *Lost and Found: Finding Self-Reliance After the Loss of a Spouse* (Collinwood Press, 2001).

Notes

Chapter Three
Government Funding of Long Term Care

Medicare, Medicaid, and a myriad of other long term care assistance programs have been enacted piecemeal over a number of years and have thus created a confusing patchwork of programs and eligibility categories. Add the various programs initiated by the states, and the numerous for profit and non-profit organizations that offer assistance and funding, and you have a system that is extremely fragmented, overlapping, and difficult to navigate. That said, the government (state and federal) pays for more than half of the cost of long term care in this country. Medicare and Medicaid are the primary programs covering long term care, with Medicaid carrying the bulk of the load, especially when it comes to nursing home care. Medicare – the federal program funded largely by payroll taxes – plays a substantial role in funding skilled home health services, but does not cover assistance with ADLs such as dressing, bathing, toileting and eating. At roughly 13%, Medicare is a much larger payer of long term nursing home care than most people realize. Despite the fact that Medicaid has a strong institutional bias, it does – to a lesser extent – cover home health services for the financially needy. Michigan funds some non-medical home care services for the financially and medically needy through its Home Help Program (administered by the Department of Health Services (DHS)) and the Older Americans Act and Older Michiganians Act (federal and state funded programs administered by the Area Agencies on Aging). The Veterans Administration also offers long term care benefits for veterans. The following is a summary of Medicare and Medicaid coverage for nursing home and in-home care.

Medicare

Medicare is the national health insurance program that covers your health care needs if you are at least 65 years of age (or younger and deemed "disabled"). Medicare may pay for help with ADLs (sometimes called "personal services") such bathing and dressing *if* you require skilled nursing home care, but will not pay for such services if skilled care is not required, and does not cover help with IADLs (such as housekeeping and shopping) under any circumstances.

Nursing Home Care

Medicare nursing home coverage is limited to skilled care in a Medicare certified facility for up to 100 days. The first twenty days are covered in full; Medicare covers days 21 through 100 to the extent the cost exceeds $114 per day. To be covered:

- The nursing home stay must follow (within 30 days) a hospital stay of at least three consecutive days;
- The treatment received in the nursing home must be related to the hospital stay; and
- A physician must certify that skilled nursing or rehabilitative services are required on a daily basis.

During your 100-day stay, the nursing home is required to regularly review your condition to determine if you still need skilled care on a daily basis. If at any time during your first 100 days you no longer need skilled care, Medicare will terminate coverage. In that case, the nursing home must give you a written notice explaining its decision to terminate coverage and explaining your appeal rights.

See Chapter Five for a detailed discussion of Medicare nursing home coverage. Answers to your Medicare questions are available from Michigan's Medicare Medicaid Assistance Program (MMAP), described below.

In-Home Care

Medicare is the primary provider of in-home skilled nursing care and other home health services for rehabilitative purposes. Home health care is covered under Medicare Part A if:

- It is prescribed by a physician;
- The services are provided by a Medicare certified home health agency (HHA);
- It follows a hospital stay of at least three consecutive days;
- The home health services are commenced within 14 days of the hospital discharge;
- It involves part time or intermittent (less than 8 hours/day, 28 hours/week) skilled nursing care, home health aide, or therapy; and
- The patient is homebound.

As with nursing home coverage, Medicare covers home care only for so long as it is determined that you need skilled services on a daily basis. Once you are eligible, the HHA bills Medicare directly much the same way as doctors bill Medicare for their services. Be careful to choose a Medicare certified home health care agency since they are the only ones eligible to receive Medicare payments. Many families find the homebound restriction burdensome since they can't take their elder anywhere, but it's the price for Medicare paying the home healthcare bill. Agencies that don't take the homebound restrictions seriously can be targeted for fraud or abuse. Medicare covers only part-time home health services, not personal care, assistance with meals, or transportation.

Unfortunately, in recent years, Medicare has limited the amount of reimbursement allocated to home care. Medicare home health visits per user declined in every state between 1993 and 2002. During this same period, the average number of Medicare home visits in the U.S. declined by 47%.

Excellent information about Medicare home health care, including denials of coverage, is available from the Center for Medicare Advocacy: www.medicareadvocacy.org. Currently, Michigan does not license HHAs, but Medicare certified home health agencies are listed on www.medicare.gov (click on "Home Health Compare") by state, county, and ZIP code. Your hospital discharge planner or private geriatric care manager should be able to recommend a Medicare certified HHA in your area. You may check out the quality of an HHA through the Joint Commission of Accreditation of Heath-care Organizations at www.jcaho.org; Community Health Accreditation Program (800) 656-9656 www.chapinc.org; and the National Association of Home Care www.nahc.org.

Medicaid

Medicaid is the government health program for the financially and medically needy. It provides long term care services to elderly and non-elderly persons with disabilities. Medicaid is basically a welfare benefit administered by the state that is federally overseen. The Michigan Department of Community Health (MDCH) runs Michigan's Medicaid program, with the Department of Health Services (DHS) handling applications and making financial eligibility determinations. Michigan funds approximately 43% of the Medicaid budget with the federal government kicking in the remaining 57%. Medicaid began paying for nursing home costs in 1965.

Nursing Home Care

Nationally, nearly 60% of those in nursing homes have Medicaid as their primary source of payment. Medicaid pays at least part of the bill for two out of every three nursing home residents. Of total national spending on long term care, Medicaid accounted for 43% of spending. In 2002, Michigan ranked 10th in the county with 41,547 nursing facility residents, 66.5 percent of whom had Medicaid as their primary payer (ranking 22nd in the county) with only 14.3 percent having Medicare as the primary payer (ranked 7th in the country).

Medicaid pays for the cost of your nursing home care if:

- You are at least age 65;
- You are found medically eligible under the state's Nursing Facility Level of Care Criteria (effective November, 2004; see https://sso.state.mi.us./);
- The nursing home is Medicaid certified; and
- You meet the strict income and asset tests described in Chapter Five.

Once eligible, Medicaid will pay for the full cost of your nursing home care over and above your *patient pay amount* (basically, all of your income, less allowance for Medicare premiums and a possible spousal stipend).

Effective November 1, 2004, Michigan adopted more stringent *medical* eligibility rules. The new rules replace the old eligibility requirement that a doctor's recommendation was all that was needed to establish medical (functional) eligibility for Medicaid's long term care benefits. Now, to qualify for Medicaid (the new rules do not apply to Medicare) long term care benefits – whether provided in a nursing home *or* through MI Choice – you must pass through one of seven *doors*. The rules establish seven separate ways to become medically eligible for Medicaid. A sufficient amount of need in any one of the following seven areas will qualify you for Medicaid: 1. Activities of Daily Living; 2. Physician Involvement; 3. Skilled Rehabilitation Therapies; 4. Service Dependency; 5. Cognitive Performance; 6. Treatments and Conditions; and 7. Behavior. If you are unable to meet any of the seven thresholds, you may seek an exception to the rules based on hardship. The state's principal reason for passing the new rules is to keep people out of nursing homes and off the Medicaid rolls. The state estimates that the new rules will reduce the number of medically eligible nursing home applicants from eight to twelve percent. We may see more of this kind of cost cutting as Michigan attempts to balance its budget.

In-Home Care

Historically, Medicaid has provided only minimal access and limited funding to home health care. All states are required to provide institutional services, but not home health care. Accordingly, states have provided home care as an optional benefit or through a waiver program. Michigan provides Medicaid in-home services through its waiver program, MI Choice, discussed below. As a result of the high demand for home health care and extremely limited funding, Medicaid home health services are extremely difficult to obtain and almost always have waiting lists.

When available, Medicaid's home health care benefit covers part-time and intermittent services similar to those provided by Medicare. Unlike Medicare, individuals need not be homebound (but they do need to meet the same functional/medical eligibility rules as required for nursing home admission), nor does the care need to follow a hospital stay. Due to limited funding, Medicaid home health benefits are subject to rigorous financial criteria – even more restrictive than Medicaid eligibility for nursing home care – and are therefore extremely difficult to obtain. Consequently, Medicaid home health benefits have dropped significantly in Michigan in recent years. Rather than in-home health services, Medicaid agencies prefer the in-home care service waiver program known as *MI Choice.*

MI Choice (pronounced "my" choice)

All states, including Michigan, offer what are called waivered services. Essentially, the state can use Medicaid dollars to pay for certain kinds of home care without following guidelines established by the federal government. Michigan's waiver program – Medicaid Home and Community Based Services Waiver for the Elderly and Disabled (HCBS) – is commonly known as MI Choice. It is designed for those who require nursing home level services but wish to remain in their own home. Although MI Choice providers cannot spend, on average, more than $34 (2005) per day in services for MI Choice participants, the services provided under MI Choice coupled with help from family members can make home care possible for those who would otherwise be institutionalized.

Waiver agents who, for the most part, are available through your local Area Agency on Aging, administer MI Choice. MI Choice offers a broad range of non-medical in-home and community based services including: personal care (such as bathing, dressing, and eating assistance), respite care (short-term relief for family caregivers provided at home, in an institution, or an adult day care center), homemaker and chore services, and transportation.

To be eligible, you must meet Medicaid asset eligibility requirements, the new Nursing Facility Level of Care Criteria *and* your monthly income cannot exceed $1,737 (2005). In practice, eligibility for the MI Choice program is more stringent than eligibility for Medicaid nursing home care.

While the state's cost for nursing home has nearly doubled in the past decade with an average current cost of $116 per person per day, average care costs under the MI Choice program have remained at $43 per person per day ($34 allocated to patient care and $9 to administrative). Despite its obvious benefits, the MI Choice program has been crippled by budgetary cuts. With its funding currently capped at $100 million (statewide), the number of people enrolled in the program has declined from a high of 15,000 in 2001 to about 7,500 today. As a result of the current low funding levels and high demand, new applicants face waiting periods of up to two years for MI Choice services.

Despite recent cutbacks, advocates of the MI Choice program remain hopeful. Similar waiver programs in Oregon, Washington, Colorado, Vermont and Arizona have succeeded in shifting the bulk of their states' long term care dollars to home care and assisted living. By contrast, the institutional bias remains strong in Michigan with institutional care receiving the bulk of the funding at more than 75 percent of all Medicaid long term care dollars.

Miscellaneous Programs
Home Help Program

The Home Help Program funded by the Michigan Department of Community Health (MDCH) and administered by the Department of Health Services (DHS), pays a small stipend to service providers chosen by program participants, typically friends and family members. The applicant must be receiving Social Security Income and be eligible for Medicaid. Participants in the MI Choice program are eligible for the Home Help Program with a doctor's certification. The Home Help Program is a very large program that covers Medicaid eligible participants with extremely low income. You apply for adult home help services at your local DHS office.

The Michigan Aging Services System (MASS)

Many in-home services programs such as home delivered meals, homemaker and home chore services, respite care and adult day care are provided through MASS. Participants are not charged for these services but are encouraged to make contributions. See www.miseniors.net for more details.

Program of All-inclusive Care for the Elderly (PACE)

PACE is basically an adult day care program where partici-pants receive personal care services and limited medical care. PACE arranges for transportation to its site for activities

Monday through Friday each week. Medicare and state Medicaid programs pay each site a monthly amount that must cover all participants and services. If you are already eligible for Medicaid, there is no additional charge for PACE. Unfortunately, due to limited funding, Michigan's PACE program covers only 200 participants statewide and is available only through Henry Ford Hospital in Detroit. Contact the Center for Senior Independence at (313) 653-2020. Visit the national PACE Web site: www.cms.hhs.gov/pace/.

Veterans Benefits

If you qualify for a VA pension, the Veterans Administration will increase your monthly pension if you are homebound or need long term care. The increased pension may be used for home care, medical equipment, assisted living (called *domiciliary* care), and even nursing home care. See the Department of Veteran Affairs Web site: www.va.gove for more information on VA programs, benefits and services.

Long Term Care Summary

Type	Help with activities of daily living	Help with additional services	Medicare Coverage	Medicaid Coverage
Independent Living Communities and Senior Apartments	No	Yes, on a fee basis	No	No
Subsidized senior housing	No	Minimal	Yes	No
Home Care	Yes	Yes	Skilled care only for so long as medically necessary	Limited to MI Choice for non-medical assistance
MI Choice	Yes	Yes	No	MI Choice is a Medicaid program
Adult Day Care	Yes	Yes	No	No, except under PACE
Assisted living	Yes	Yes	No	No
Continuing Care Retirement Community(CCRC)	Yes	Yes	Nursing home only. Limited to 100 days	No
Adult Foster Care (AFC)	Yes	Yes	No	Yes, but difficult to qualify
Homes For the Aged (HFA)	Yes	Yes	No	Yes, but difficult to qualify
Nursing home	Yes	Yes	Limited to 100 days if you qualify	Yes, if you qualify
Hospice	Yes	Yes	Yes	Yes

Chapter Four
Getting Help

You should seek professional help to properly assess your needs and help you choose among the myriad of long term care options – especially if you wish to age in place. The likely fact that you haven't been through this process before, coupled with the typical urgency that normally accompanies long term care placement decisions, dictates that you get help. Your local Area Agency on Aging, ombudsman, private geriatric case manager, and hospital discharge planner are excellent resources to assist you in sorting through your options. Your local AAA is the place to start; they have the greatest resources and expertise. Your local ombudsman can help you choose the best nursing home for your needs. Private geriatric care managers can be used to supplement the services provided by your local AAA. Hospital discharge planners are a short-term last resort option when you are being discharged from a hospital and you have not done advance planning. All but hospital discharge planners offer *care management* to help you coordinate home care and other needed services where multiple services and agencies are involved.

Area Agency on Aging

Your local Area Agency on Aging (AAA) is the best place to begin. AAAs were established under the Older Americans Act of 1973. Area Agencies on Aging provide information and referrals to help you find the services you need. The services offered by the various AAA offices differ, but all are great sources of information. Each offers care management to assist you in coordinating home care (sometimes for a fee), most act as the waiver agent for the MI Choice program, and all can help you locate senior subsidized housing. AAA management services are usually free or low cost for those who qualify. Eligibility for AAA assistance is based on the amount of help and care you need, not your income. Even if you are ineligible for care management services, the AAA should be able to direct you to other services that can help meet your needs.

Area Agencies on Aging fund local organizations to deliver personal care and homemaker services to older adults in need. Services are generally offered on a part-time basis, typically a few hours each week. The services are usually free or offered at very reduced costs, although donations are accepted. Waiting lists for AAA services are common.

The Michigan Department of Community Health (MDCH) Office of Services to the Aging sponsors an excellent Web site: www.miseniors.net. For assistance with ADLs see the DHS Web site: www.michigan.gov/fia. Call the Elder Care Locater at 1-800-677-1116 for AAAs across the country. A list of the AAA offices in Michigan by county is reproduced in Appendix A of this book.

Ombudsman Program

The Michigan long term care ombudsman program, administered in most districts in Michigan by Citizens for Better Care, advocates for residents of long term care facilities. They address complaints made by or on behalf of residents and work to help to resolve them. The ombudsman program helps consumers shop for long term care services by advising them on how to find, select and pay for care that meets their needs. Ombudsmen regularly visit nursing home facilities, and as a result are a very good source of general information. Although they don't rank nursing homes, they can tell you the number and nature of the complaints they have received about a particular nursing home, and will steer you away from the bad ones. Long term care ombudsman services are confidential and free. Ombudsmen advocate, educate, provide practical information and give referrals. They also regulate licensed adult foster care homes (AFC) and homes for the aged. Ombudsman services in Michigan are listed in Appendix B.

The Citizens for Better Care Web site, www.cbcmi.org, provides valuable information about nursing homes and advocacy in Michigan. Citizens for Better Care also publishes *The Michigan Long Term Care Companion,* a 387 page book that covers all aspects of obtaining quality long term care in Michigan which you can order for $25.00 by calling (313) 832-6387.

Private Geriatric Care Manager

Geriatric care managers typically charge an up-front initial assessment fee and work by the hour thereafter to assist you in arranging and monitoring short or long term care (called *case management*). Typically, the process starts with an on-site *assessment and evaluation* visit to your home. Geriatric care managers typically have the hands-on experience to help you locate qualified home care, assisted living and nursing home providers in your area. Michigan does not currently regulate or license geriatric care managers, so it is important to ask for their educational background and experience (you're looking for nursing, social work, and gerontology backgrounds), and get references (especially of clients they have served). Your local AAA office or hospital discharge planner can give you a list of the geriatric care managers in your area.

The National Association of Professional Geriatric Care Managers, (520) 881-8008, Fax (520) 325-7925 Web site: www.caremanager.org can help you identify qualified professional geriatric care managers in your area. Also visit www.careguide.com.

Hospital Discharge Planner

Discharge planners are hospital employees who arrange hospital aftercare. They facilitate the hospital discharge process by identifying basic patient needs and arranging appropriate in-home, rehabilitative, or nursing home care. The role of the discharge planner has become more important as patients are being discharged "sicker and quicker." Patients are often too sick to go home, but for insurance reimbursement purposes must leave the hospital (but see the three-day MPRO appeal process below).

Hospital discharge planners work for the hospital, and basically do what is best for their employer. Their principal duty is to discharge you as soon as possible. If you have good insurance, they may recommend their own nursing facility, and if you don't, or if you have limited resources, they may recommend the first available facility irrespective of the quality of care. Hospital discharge planners have a heavy case load, and rarely have the time to work with you to arrange home care or adult day care. Contact your local AAA or private geriatric care manager if you believe you are not getting the service you require.

The best advice is to plan ahead. Don't wait until you experience an illness or injury to begin looking at your alternatives. Hospital discharge planners don't have the time or the incentive to create a plan that gives you the greatest autonomy; their job is to get you out of the hospital. If you want to age in place, you must plan for your own future.

If you believe you are being discharged from the hospital prematurely, you may use your appeal rights under Medicare to stay an extra three days – without paying for it. To do so, you must appeal your discharge by contacting the Michigan Peer Review Organization (MPRO) (free of charge) at 22670 Haggerty Rd., Suite 100, Farmington Hills, Michigan 48335-2611 (800) 365-5899 or Website: www.mpro.org by noon of the first working day after you receive what is called the Hospital-Issued Notice of Non-coverage (HINN). The MPRO is required to make a decision on your appeal by the end of the next business day. Even if the MPRO agrees with the hospital, you will not be responsible for hospital charges until noon of the day after you receive the MPRO's decision. Thus, even in the worst case scenario, you have given yourself three extra days of covered hospital care to more thoroughly and thoughtfully examine your long term care options.

Medicare Medicaid Assistance Program (MMAP)

MMAP is a free counseling service for Medicare/Medicaid beneficiaries and caregivers. By calling 1-800-803-7174, you will be automatically linked with a MMAP (pronounced "map") counselor in your area who can help you understand doctor and hospital bills, Medicare and Medicaid eligibility and coverage, claims and appeals, as well as help you enroll in Medicare savings programs. They will review Medicare supplemental insurance needs, identify resources for prescription drug assistance, explore long term care financing options including long term care insurance, and identify and report Medicare/Medicaid fraud and abuse.

Single Point of Entry

Governor Granholm has established the Long Term Care Task Force to investigate ways to make the long term care delivery system in Michigan more efficient and cost effective. The Task Force has recommended a *single point of entry* to allow easier access to Medicaid benefits. A single point of entry – which will likely be a phone number and Web site – will allow all Michigan residents simple entry into the current maze of Medicaid long term care programs. Callers will be directed to their local AAA office where they will be assessed and directed to programs for which they qualify.

Other Resources

See www.michigan.gov/ltc for information on long term care in Michigan including programs administered by the Department of Health Services (DHS). The site allows you to search for nursing homes in Michigan by county, city, or ZIP code.

The Michigan Department of Community Health (MDCH) Office of Services to the Aging sponsors an excellent Web site: www.miseniors.net that supplies information about services administered by the aging network and the MDCH. Under Resource Directory, you can search for services or agencies dealing with every imaginable long term care need.

See www.medicare.gov, the official U.S. Web site for Medicare. Select "Long Term Care." The Web site lists nursing homes by city and zip code and provides general information about every Medicare and Medicaid certified nursing home in the country including nursing home inspection results, the number of nursing home staff, and resident information. Their Web site also provides access to several interactive databases, which offer detailed comparison information on nursing homes, Medicare health care plans, and Medigap policies by State or ZIP Code.

www.AlternativesForSeniors.com publishes a free booklet outlining the various senior housing and services in Southeast Michigan. The publication describes the services available at various home care, adult day care, senior apartments, retirement communities, assisted living, Alzheimer's/Dementia, and nursing centers in Southeast Michigan. www.alternativesforseniors.com. 1 (800) 350 0770.

www.aarp.org/internetresources.com is a free database, sponsored by AARP, that includes 600 Web sites. It includes internet information from federal and state agencies on community services, Social Security, long term care, housing, employment, legal issues, retirement, medical conditions, Medicare and Medicaid, as well as the Web sites of aging organizations from around the world.

The American Association of Homes and Services for the Aging (AAHSA) offers a series of free "Consumer Tips" on finding home and community services, assisted living facilities, nursing homes, and continuing care retirement communities by State or ZIP Code. See www.aahsa.org (Select "Consumers")

Notes

Chapter Five
Medicare and Medicaid Eligibility

The average cost of a year in a nursing home in Michigan is approximately $64,404 (2005), equating to $177 per day. Further, according to the State of Michigan Web site, www.Michigan.gov, roughly fifty percent of those age 65 or older will spend some time in a nursing home. The average nursing home stay is nineteen months, with about thirty three percent of residents spending three months or more, about twenty five percent spending an average of a year, and a little less than ten percent spending five or more *years.*

The high cost of skilled nursing care is of special concern to *community spouses,* that is, the non-institutionalized spouse of a skilled nursing care patient. This Chapter Five focuses on the sources of funding for the payment of long term care: Medicare, private pay, and Medicaid.

Medicare

Medicare is the federal government health insurance program for seniors (age 65 and older), the disabled (under age 65), and individuals (any age) who have permanent kidney failure. With respect to long term care, Medicare covers medical needs, but not custodial care such as assistance with ADLs. Medicare is not need based, and therefore pays for all necessary medical treatment regardless of your financial status.

Medicare covers only the first 100 days of a nursing home stay; paying 100% percent of the cost of the first 20 days, and the cost of the remaining 80 days only to the extent that it *exceeds* $114 per day. To be eligible for Medicare coverage, the stay must be in an approved skilled nursing facility that immediately follows a hospital stay of at least three days. Further, to be eligible, you must enter the skilled nursing facility within 30 days of your discharge from the hospital, and the skilled nursing facility stay must be for the same reason as the hospitalization. Slightly augmented coverage may be provided under private *medigap* coverage during the 100-day period, but medigap coverage does not otherwise cover long term care. Medicare covers the full cost of in-home skilled nursing home care, and 80% of durable medical equipment if the requirements outlined in Chapter Three are met, namely that it be prescribed by a physician, is part time and intermittent, and the patient is homebound.

Medicare consists of two parts: Part A covers inpatient hospital care as well as a portion of the first 100 days of a patient's stay in a skilled nursing facility, home health care following a hospital stay, and hospice care. Part B of Medicare covers doctor's services, medical services, supplies, and other services not covered by Part A. While Part A is free to eligible workers (Part A is financed during your working years by the 1.45% Medicare tax on all earned income), Part B coverage requires that you pay a monthly premium (for 2005, the basic Part B premium is $78.20 per month), which is automatically deducted from your monthly Social Security check if you receive benefits. If you elect to defer receipt of Social Security retirement benefits beyond age 65, you may make quarterly Part B premium payments directly to the Social Security Administration. Part B should not be viewed as optional. Although participation is elective (you must pay premiums), Part B coverage is an essential part of your personal medical plan.

The coverage offered under Medicare Part A and B leaves coverage gaps in the form of limitations on prescription coverage, deductibles, and co-pays. The private sector has responded to fill the gaps in Medicare coverage by offering private health insurance that covers medical costs not covered by Medicare. Not surprisingly, these policies have come to be known as *Medigap* policies.

Medicare's coverage of long term care can be summarized as follows:

Summary of Medicare Skilled Nursing Facility Coverage

Benefit	Medicare Pays	You Pay
First 20 days of Care	100% of Approved Amount	None of approved amount, but all of non-approved amount
Next 80 days of care	Only above $114 a day	Up to $114 a day
Beyond 100 days	Nothing	All Costs

Summary of Medicare In-Home Coverage

Benefit	Medicare Pays	You Pay
Home Health Care	Unlimited, if eligibility requirements discussed in Chapter Three are met and is under physician's treatment plan	20% of amount of durable medical equipment

Private Pay

The cost of long term care falls to the individual after Medicare benefits are exhausted (if eligible at all). You must continue to pay privately until you have sufficiently exhausted your assets to become eligible for Medicaid. Individuals with adequate means who enjoy good health may insure against the possibility of an extended nursing home stay by purchasing long term care insurance (see Chapter Eight).

Medicaid

Medicaid is a federally funded, state-administered welfare program restricted to the financially indigent. The Medicaid program is need based, providing benefits only to those who demonstrate financial need (determined by federal guidelines modified to a certain extent by the state). To qualify, all of your income must be applied to your care and you cannot have more than a limited amount of cash or other available assets. If you have excess assets, you'll be required to use them up before coverage begins.

The Medicaid program is implemented by each state individually. The federal government is involved because it reimburses the state for a substantial portion of Medicaid benefits paid to its citizens, provided the state's Medicaid program meets the prescribed federal guidelines. Hence, the states tend to follow the dictates of the federal government.

Even though Medicaid is need based, in Chapter Six we will demonstrate how you can restructure your assets to qualify for benefits without going broke. To qualify for Medicaid you must have exhausted substantially all of your non-exempt assets. You may be tempted to simply gift your assets to family members. This process, called "divestment," can be perilous when done without the counsel of a qualified elder law attorney.

Eligibility

You are eligible for Medicaid if you are at least age 65, demonstrate financial need, pass through one of the seven medical *eligibility doors,* and follow the procedures for applying for Medicaid. Financial need is broken into two parts: income and assets.

Income Test

If medical expenses exceed income, then the income test is met. Income is defined as both earned and unearned income including interest, dividends, rents, Social Security benefits and retirement benefits. You are not eligible for Medicaid if your income *exceeds* the monthly private pay rate for the nursing home ($5,367 in 2005). It is important to note that income of the community spouse is *not* counted as available to the institutionalized spouse. If the income test is met, you then look at the asset test.

Asset Test

An *unmarried* applicant may have no more than $2,000 of *countable* (as opposed to *excluded* or *exempt*) assets. Counted assets include all assets including IRAs, the cash value of life insurance, stocks, and savings bonds. If you have countable assets in excess of $2,000, your Medicaid application will be denied. If you are married, your spouse (*community spouse*) may keep all exempt assets plus an extra amount, known as the *community spouse resource allowance* (CSRA).

Married Applicant

When determining eligibility for Medicaid, all assets owned in your own name, in your spouse's name, or together with your spouse are counted as your assets. However, special relief is granted to the community spouse to prevent spousal impoverishment. The community spouse is entitled to a *community spouse resource allowance* (CSRA), which is the greater of $19,032 (2005) or one-half (1/2) of the countable assets (as reported on the Asset Declaration Form as of the *snapshot date*) not to exceed $95,160 (2005). If both spouses are in a nursing home, you are each treated as a single person and your counted assets may not exceed $3,000.

For example: Dee Mensha and her husband Bob own a home valued at $200,000 and have $100,000 in liquid assets. Their countable assets are only $100,000 since their home is exempt. Bob's community spouse resource allowance is $50,000. Dee will not be eligible for Medicaid until she spends down $48,000 (remember she gets to keep $2,000).

Jointly Held Assets

The treatment of jointly held assets under Medicaid is confusing. Assets held jointly between a husband and wife are considered to be totally available to the applicant spouse and are therefore fully included in his assets. In those cases where assets are jointly owned with someone other than a spouse (including assets held as *tenants in common*), the rules differentiate between *cash assets* (bank accounts, certificates of deposit and annuities) and *all other joint assets*. You are deemed to own one hundred percent of the cash assets unless it can be proven that the other joint tenants actually contributed to the account from their separate funds. Non-cash joint accounts (including real estate, stocks, promissory notes, and mutual funds) are deemed owned proportionately by the joint tenants. For example, if there are three people on the account or a parcel of real estate, you are deemed to own one-third of the account. A divestment occurs when a non-cash joint account is created with a non-spouse within the look-back period. In other words, it is treated as a gift. Once created, the non-cash joint account would be considered *unavailable* to you and therefore not part of your assets *if* the other joint tenants refuse to release or liquidate the joint asset. However, you could later face a period of disqualification if the joint tenants agree to liquidate the asset, making your proportional share of the asset available to you.

Snapshot Date

This snapshot date is the first day of a 30 consecutive day *continuous period of institutionalization*. If you are hospitalized and then go into a nursing home, the snapshot day is the first day of your admission to the hospital. If there is a break of at least thirty days between your release from the hospital and admission to the nursing home, the snapshot date will be your admission to the nursing home. Adult foster care homes, homes for the aged and home health care do not qualify as long-term care for this purpose. An Asset Declaration form (Form FIA-4574-B, reproduced at the end of this Chapter Five) must be filed reporting all property owned by either spouse individually, jointly, or jointly with other persons as of the snapshot date. The Department of Human Resources (DHS), formerly known as

Family Independence Agency (FIA), is required to issue its calculation of the community spouse resource allowance within 45 days of the date of the filing of the Asset Declaration form. The Asset Declaration form is separate from and must be filed prior to or at the same time as submission of the Medicaid application. Verification of all assets listed on the Declaration form is required, so it is important to gather all such supporting documentation (bank and brokerage account statements, etc.) reporting values *as of the snapshot date.* For example, if the snapshot date is six months prior to submission of the Asset Declaration form, supporting documentation should be as of the snapshot date and not the date of submission of the Asset Declaration form. After the Asset Declaration form has been submitted, it is necessary to keep meticulous records and documentation showing how assets are spent. Criminal penalties may apply to Medicaid fraud, so all answers must be full and truthful. Also, any new asset information must be reported within 10 days.

Couples with countable assets of less than two times the maximum CSRA [two times $95,160 (2005) or $190,320] can use the fact that the CSRA is calculated as of the snapshot date (and not the date you apply for Medicaid) to maximize their CSRA. By increasing the amount of countable assets on the snapshot date the couple can increase their CSRA.

For example: As noted in the above example, Bob Mensha's CSRA was $50,000 (one half of he and Dee's countable assets). If, instead, Dee and Bob transferred their $200,000 residence from their joint names into Dee's trust (thereby making it countable) prior to the snapshot date, their countable assets would be $300,000 rather than $100,000 and their CSRA would be $95,160 rather than $50,000. The home would then be transferred to the community spouse (not the applicant) *after* the snapshot date and prior to the filing of the Medicaid application to effectively return the residence to exempt status.

The planning technique described above requires advance planning. A hospital stay is often not anticipated. If an unexpected hospital admission is followed by a permanent transfer to a nursing home, which is not uncommon, the opportunity for a couple to gross up their countable assets by the snapshot date may be lost. However, if you have not had an opportunity to plan prior to the snapshot date, you may (if physically possible) leave the nursing home for a period of at least thirty days to acquire a new snapshot date, thereby creating a new opportunity to plan.

The CSRA is determined only once during any period of continuous institutionalization. Therefore, once you are determined to be Medicaid eligible (actually the first day of the month following the determination), the community spouse's assets are no longer relevant. The community spouse can acquire assets of any value (even win the lottery) without affecting the resident spouse's benefits.

If you believe that the CSRA is not adequate for your needs, you may request a fair hearing with the DHS to seek an increase. The request should be made at the time of the initial Medicaid application. You may also obtain a court order directing assets to be transferred to the community spouse.

Once determined, the spousal resource allowance must be transferred to the community spouse within the one year *presumed eligibility period* (see Follow Up for Married Applicants in Chapter Six). If the spousal allowance is not so transferred, it will become an asset of the nursing home spouse, thus causing disqualification.

For Example: Percy Veer enters a nursing home in February of 2005, and his wife, Sue, is allowed $50,000 (one-half of their countable assets of $100,000) as her CSRA. Seven months later, on September 7, Percy is determined to be eligible for Medicaid, and Sue still has her $50,000 allowance. On October 1, Sue inherits $200,000 from the estate of her deceased sister, increasing Sue's total assets to $250,000. Sue's CSRA and inheritance will have no effect on Percy's Medicaid benefits as long as they are transferred into Sue's name alone.

Exempt Assets

Medicaid distinguishes between countable and excluded (exempt) assets. The following assets (sometimes referred to as *excluded assets*) are not considered for purposes of the $2,000 limit:

1. An automobile of any value. If you own more than one automobile, you may choose the one you want to exempt (presumably the most expensive one). You may own an exempt auto even if you cannot drive, as long as it is used primarily for family transportation purposes (thus excluding RVs). Although an automobile of any value is technically exempt, the DHS can attack the purchase if it believes that the vehicle was purchased solely for the purpose of qualifying for Medicaid (don't buy a Ferrari).
2. One principal residence of any value ("homestead") including all contiguous land even if it crosses roads or rivers (see more about principal residences below);
3. Household goods, furniture and personal effects, including clothing and jewelry;
4. A prepaid irrevocable funeral contract not to exceed $10,257 (2005);
5. Cemetery plot;
6. Cash value of life insurance up to $1,500;
7. Income producing real property where the net income derived from rents is at least 6% of your equity (fair market value less mortgages) in the rented property; and
8. Miscellaneous other exemptions not relevant here.

Principal Residence

A principal residence loses its exempt status if it is owned in trust. However, a residence not in trust would be subject to probate. A *ladybird deed* will allow you to qualify for Medicaid and at the same time avoid probate. A ladybird deed allows you to transfer your principal residence to your trust *but* retain the right to live in the home and the power to sell it without the consent of any other party. Having retained a life interest, the home is considered your personal residence for Medicaid purposes, and will continue to qualify as your homestead for valuable property and income tax exemptions. However, at death the home is – by the terms of the ladybird deed – owned by your trust and thereby avoids probate.

Your principal residence remains exempt even if you go into a nursing home. Fearing that their home may be vandalized while they are in the nursing home, many families would prefer to rent the home rather than have it sit vacant. If rented, the net rental proceeds are considered income that is counted toward the *patient pay amount*. The following two-step strategy keeps the rental income in the family: first, rent the home for a minimal amount to a family member, who in turn rents the home to a third party for fair market value. Only the minimal rent charged to the family member becomes part of the patient pay amount. Your family member, who is working hard on your behalf overseeing your cherished family home, can keep the balance of the rent. This strategy works for two reasons: the Medicaid rules do not require you to charge fair market rent, and the 6% income rule for rental property doesn't apply to homesteads.

If your principal residence is in another state, let's say Florida, and you decide to enter a nursing home in Michigan, you may nonetheless qualify your Florida residence as your principal residence for Medicaid purposes.

Income
Patient Pay Amount

To qualify for Medicaid, your income cannot exceed the average cost of a nursing home stay as calculated by the state. If your monthly income exceeds the cost of your nursing home stay, all of your income must be used for such purpose. If your income is less than the monthly cost of the nursing home, the amount you must pay toward your nursing home care (the *patient pay amount*) must be calculated. Basically, all of your income, including Social Security, pension payments, and IRA age 70 1/2 minimum distributions is counted toward your *patient pay amount* reduced by a *personal needs allowance* of $60, and further reduced by the cost of health insurance (including vision and dental insurance).

Spousal Income Allowance

Remember, no part of your community spouse's income is required to be used to pay your nursing home costs. In fact, the community spouse is assured of a minimum allowance that will be diverted from the resident spouse's income. If necessary, the resident spouse's income will be diverted to the community spouse to bring the community spouse's income to a minimum of $1,610 per month (July 2005) but not to exceed $2,379 when the community spouse's *shelter allowance* is added. The community spouse's minimum income allowance is reduced by the community spouse's income (including pension, Social Security, interest, dividends, etc.), and increased by the amount that her rent, mortgage property taxes and utilities exceed $468 (2005).

For Example: Guy Zerr is in a nursing home. He receives monthly Social Security of $1,500 and a pension of $500. Vi, his wife, receives Social Security of $500. Guy and Vi's annual property taxes are $2,400. They pay homeowners insurance of $600 annually, and monthly utilities of $300. Guy and Vi pay $250 for Medigap health insurance. The following example illustrates Vi's income allowance and Guy's patient pay amount.

Shelter Allowance

Property Taxes	$ 200
Insurance	50
Utilities	300
Total Shelter Expenses	550
Minimum Shelter Allowance	(468)
Excess Shelter Allowance	$ 150

Spousal Allowance

Excess Shelter Allowance	$ 150
2005 Minimum Spousal Allowance	1,610
Total Allowance	1,760
Vi's Social Security	(500)
Spousal Allowance	$1,260

Patient Pay Amount

Guy's Social Security	$1,500
Guy's Pension	500
Guy's Total Income	2,000
Personal Needs Allowance	(60)
Health Insurance Premium	(250)
Spousal Allowance	(1,260)
Monthly Patient Pay Amount	$ 430

Divestment

To qualify for Medicaid you must have exhausted all but $2,000 of your counted assets. To prevent people from simply giving away all of their assets just before entering the nursing home, the law provides that certain transfers of assets for *less than fair market value* will be *counted* as part of the Medicaid applicant's assets if transferred within the *look back* period.

Divestment is the transfer of countable (i.e., non-excluded) assets for less than fair market value within the look back period. The look back period is thirty six months for outright transfers, and sixty months for transfers to trust. Divestment does not occur if countable assets are converted to exempt assets of equal value. For example, paying off the mortgage on your home, buying a new car or purchasing an irrevocable funeral arrangement does not constitute divestment.

Divestment within the look back period does *not* cause permanent disqualification from Medicaid, nor does the state of Michigan or the nursing home confiscate the transferred funds. Instead, you are disqualified from Medicaid for a period of time measured by dividing the *uncompensated value* of the transferred assets by the average monthly private pay nursing home costs published by the state. For example, if on the eve of entering a nursing home and applying for Medicaid, Greg Arius gives his son $134,175, Greg will be ineligible for Medicaid for twenty-five (25) months [$134,175 divided by the average monthly cost of long term care in Michigan ($5,367 in 2005)]. There is *no limit* on the length of disqualification resulting from divestment *within* the look back period.

Generally, the transfer of an *exempt* asset during the look back period is *not* considered a divestment. For example, a gift of your car immediately before entering the nursing home would not cause a period of disqualification. However, the transfer of your homestead within the look back period, unless the transfer is to your spouse or a disabled child, *is* considered a divestment. A transfer of your homestead to a revocable living trust, while not a divestment, does make the home a countable asset.

Failure to disclose gifted assets on the Medicaid application can result in disqualification, fines, and even criminal penalties. It's not worth it, especially when the transfer can be done legally, as we will see in Chapter Six.

For outright gifts made more than thirty-six months prior to application, and gifts in trust made more than sixty months prior to application, there is no penalty or disqualification period, *regardless* of the value of the gift. However, gifts made *within* the look back period can create a disqualification period greater than the thirty-six or sixty month look back.

> **For Example:** Helen Bakk, a single woman, gives her only asset, her $536,700 home, to her son Ty. The average private pay rate in Michigan at the time of the gift is $5,367, causing a potential disqualification period of 100 months ($536,700 divided by $5,367). If Helen waits at least 36 months (the look back period for outright gifts) to apply for Medicaid, she will be immediately eligible. If,

on the other hand, she applies for Medicaid 35 months after the gift, she is disqualified for one hundred months from the date of the original transfer!

Look Back For Transfers to Trust

You may have grave reservations about simply giving away your assets. In that case, you may choose to transfer your assets into trust in order to prevent your beneficiaries from wasting the transfer. As noted earlier, the general rule is that a longer sixty-month look back applies to transfers in trust. How the sixty-month rule works depends on the type and terms of the trust.

A transfer to a revocable living trust is simply ignored because you retain the right to get the transferred asset back at any time you choose. Therefore, no disqualification period occurs upon the creation or funding of a revocable living trust. However, a subsequent transfer from a revocable trust to a third party (other than you or your spouse) is a disqualifying transfer and subject to a look-back period of *sixty* months. A transfer to an *irrevocable trust* is not a divestment if you retain the use or enjoyment of any portion of trust principal or income (whether or not actually so used for your benefit) *but* the transferred assets remain countable. As with revocable trusts, no divestment occurs on the establishment or funding of the trust. Interestingly, transfers out of such an irrevocable trust to a third party (other than you or your spouse) results in only a thirty-six-month look back. Finally, if the trust is irrevocable and you do not retain an interest in any portion of trust principal and income, then the transfer of assets to the trust is a divestment subject to a sixty-month look back period. When the sixty-month look back applies, transfers *out* of the trust to third parties are not subject to any look back. The trust rules can be summarized as follows:

Transfer to:	Divestment	Look back commences	Look back period
Revocable trust	No	When assets transferred out of trust	60 months
Irrevocable trust w/no retained right to principal or income	Yes	When trust funded	60 months
Irrevocable trust w/retained right to principal or income	No	When assets transferred out of trust	36 months

ASSETS DECLARATION
PATIENT AND SPOUSE
Michigan Department of Social Services

FOR OFFICE USE ONLY			
Case Name			
Case Number			
County	District	Unit	Worker

PLEASE PRINT

Patient's Name *(First, Middle, Last)*	Phone No. of Nursing Home	Spouse's Name *(First, Middle, Last)*	Spouse's Phone Number
Address of Nursing Home *(Number, Street, Rural Route)*		Spouse's Address *(Number, Street, Rural Route)*	
City / State / Zip Code		City / State / Zip Code	
Patient's Birthdate *(Mo/Day/Yr)*	Patient's Social Security Number	Spouse's Birthdate *(Mo/Day/Yr)*	Spouse's Social Security Number

This form asks questions about the property or assets owned by you and/or your spouse. This information is needed to determine your eligibility for Medicaid and the amount of assets that can be protected for the benefit of your spouse.

Answer the following questions by providing information about all assets owned by you and/or your spouse as of _____. Include assets you owned jointly with your spouse, family or other persons.

ASSETS

Do you and/or your spouse have any of the following? Each item must be answered YES or NO. Check yes even if the item is jointly owned. "Jointly owned" means your name and someone else's name is listed on the asset. For example, your name is not the only name listed on an account or on a registration or title to property.

	YES	NO	Amount or Value		YES	NO	Amount or Value
1. Cash on Hand or in a Safety Deposit Box	☐	☐	$	11. Home	☐	☐	$
2. Cash in a Patient Trust Fund	☐	☐	$	12. Land or Buildings Other Than Your Home	☐	☐	$
3. Savings Bonds	☐	☐	$	13. Cars, Pick-Ups or Trucks	☐	☐	$
4. Money Market Funds	☐	☐	$	14. Other Vehicles such as Motorhomes, Campers, Boats, Trailers, Snowmobiles, Motorcycles	☐	☐	$
5. IRA or KEOGH Accounts	☐	☐	$	15. Mortgage or Land Contracts Payable to You	☐	☐	$
6. Trust Funds	☐	☐	$	16. Farm Equipment, Livestock, or Crops	☐	☐	$
7. Stocks or Bonds or Any Account With a Stockbroker	☐	☐	$	17. Tools and Equipment	☐	☐	$
8. Notes or Contracts Payable to You	☐	☐	$	18. Funeral Contract	☐	☐	$
9. Life Insurance	☐	☐	$	19. Burial Trust Funds	☐	☐	$
10. Life Estate	☐	☐	$	20. Burial Plots	☐	☐	$

AUTHORITY: 42 CFR Part 435.
COMPLETION: Voluntary.
PENALTY: No Medicaid.

The Department of Social Services will not discriminate against any individual or group because of race, sex, religion, age, national origin, color, marital status, disability or political beliefs.

DSS-4574B (Rev. 3-94) Previous edition obsolete.

ASSETS

COMPLETE THIS PAGE BY CHECKING YES OR NO OR WRITING IN THE ANSWER.

The Department of Social Services may check records with banks, credit unions, and savings and loans concerning any accounts that you may have. These accounts may be verified by computer cross-checking.

1. Is your name, or your spouse's name, on one or more checking accounts in any bank, credit union or savings and loan?
   ☐ YES   ☐ NO

2. Is your name, or your spouse's name, on one or more savings accounts or Certificates of Deposit in any bank, credit union or savings and loan?
   ☐ YES   ☐ NO

3. List each account, the name and address where the account is located, the account number and the balance in the account. Include all accounts, even those held jointly with other persons, those with small balances, Christmas clubs and accounts used for direct deposit. List the name of every person on the account.

CHECKING ACCOUNTS

Name(s) on the Account	Name and Address of Bank, Credit Union, or Savings and Loan	Account Number	Balance	
A.				
B.				
C.				

SAVINGS ACCOUNTS OR CERTIFICATES OF DEPOSIT

Name(s) on the Account	Name and Address of Bank, Credit Union, or Savings and Loan	Account Number	Balance	
A.				
B.				
C.				
D.				

4. Do you have an account that is not listed above?   ☐ YES   ☐ NO

5. Have you, your spouse or someone acting for either of you ever put any money, income, a lawsuit settlement or assets in a trust, annuity or similar device?   ☐ YES   ☐ NO

6. Do you have any other assets not already listed on this form?   ☐ YES   ☐ NO

   If yes, explain: _____

AFFIDAVIT

I swear or affirm that all the information that I have written on this form or told to a caseworker is true. I understand that I can be prosecuted for perjury if I have intentionally given false information. I also know that I may be asked to show proof of any information I have given. I also know that if I have intentionally left out any information or if I have given false information, which causes me to receive assistance I am not entitled to or more assistance than I am entitled to, I can be prosecuted for fraud.

Signature (Patient or Authorized Representative)		Date (Month, Day, Year)
Two Witnesses Only If Signed by Mark **X**	Signature of First Witness	Signature of Second Witness

NOTE: If you are not an authorized representative but you helped complete this application, print your name and phone number where you may be reached.

Name (First, Middle, Last)	Phone Number

DSS-4574B (Rev. 3-94) (Back)

Notes

Chapter Six
Medicaid Planning Techniques and Strategies

There are a number of techniques and strategies to preserve your estate in the event you need long term nursing home care:

Gifting

We don't advise you to simply give your assets away to qualify for Medicaid. Although many of the strategies discussed in this Chapter Six involve some form of gifting, you should not make gifts in anticipation of needing long term care without the advice of a competent elder law attorney. A gift of countable assets (unless to a spouse) within the look back period is a *divestment* that will result in Medicaid disqualification for a period of months determined by dividing the value of the gift by the average monthly cost of a nursing home stay ($5,367 in 2005).

$$\frac{\text{Value of gift}}{5,367} = \text{months of disqualification}$$

Gifting has a number of ancillary consequences – including gift and income tax issues and loss of control – that must be examined. Even though the Medicaid savings almost always outweigh these issues, you should know the full consequences of your actions. An elder law attorney can help you weigh the income and gift tax consequences of making gifts. Gifts of more than $11,000 in one year to any one beneficiary reduce your one million dollar gift tax exemption and will require the filing of a federal gift tax return (Form 709). Also, the recipient of a gift receives a *carryover basis,* and therefore loses the favorable *stepped-up basis* income tax treatment for assets received at death.

Convert Countable Assets to Exempt Assets

A simple way to reduce your countable assets is to convert them to exempt assets. Changing assets from countable to exempt is not considered a transfer and therefore does not trigger a period of disqualification. Countable liquid assets could be used to pay off the mortgage on your exempt residence, purchase a car, prepay funeral bills, or to improve your residence (new roof, furnace, air conditioning, sun room, etc.). It is advisable to pay off all debts. The DHS does not allow a deduction for debts, even debts secured by exempt assets.

If you don't own a home, consider purchasing one with countable assets. The home will be exempt if you can prove that you or your spouse actually moved into the home and used it as your principal residence. If you are married, the home should be purchased in the community spouse's name so that if it is sold at a later date the proceeds will not be counted as part of the applicant spouse's assets. Countable assets should be converted to exempt assets *after* the snapshot date (for married applicants), and in all events *prior* to the filing of the Medicaid application.

Pay Family Members for Service

Generally, it is permissible under the Medicaid rules to pay friends and family members for personal services, housekeeping, home repair, and transportation. The law provides that payment for services to a "non-legally responsible person" are permissible (and not a transfer of counted assets) if commensurate with the services rendered. We recommend that you enter into a written *caregiver agreement* with your friend or family member to document the services to be rendered and the compensation to be paid. You will find a written agreement useful in many ways: to support the payments for Medicaid purposes, to preserve the caregiver's claim for payment, to protect you from potential gouging, and to justify the payments to jealous family members.

Serial Divestment

Serial divestment is a technique that allows you to give away the largest possible amount, during the look back period, while incurring the shortest possible disqualification period. In serial divestment, you make monthly gifts to beneficiaries of your choosing in an amount that is slightly less than two times the average monthly nursing home cost. For example, if the average monthly nursing home cost is $5,367 (2005), a monthly gift of $10,000 results in a *one month* period of disqualification that expires on the last day of the calendar month in which the gift was completed. Serial divestment works for the following reasons:

- Michigan does not recognize partial periods of disqualification and rounds fractions down to the next whole number of months. A $10,000 gift results in a 1.86 month period of disqualification which is rounded *down* to 1 month; and
- Each calendar month is a *new* gifting period for computing gifts. So, for example, a gift of $10,000 (which rounds down to a one month period of disqualification) on March 25th would cause disqualification for the month of March *only*. Gifts of $10,000 can be made each month, never causing a period of disqualification that exceeds 30 days.

Serial divestment is most appropriate if you are unmarried (married applicants will likely prefer use of the spousal annuity trust described below), and must be completed *before* the Medicaid application is filed. Naturally, you must be comfortable parting with your hard earned assets. If you are concerned that your beneficiaries will waste your monthly divestments, you may contribute them to an irrevocable trust (of which you are neither the beneficiary or trustee). Finally, although serial divestment can dramatically accelerate Medicaid eligibility, it usually takes several months if not years to complete. If you become disabled during the divestment process, your family may continue divesting on your behalf using the Medicaid friendly durable power of attorney (see Chapter One) you created exactly for such purpose.

Spousal Annuity Trust

A spousal annuity trust is an irrevocable trust that holds assets *solely for the benefit of* the community spouse during the community spouse's lifetime. Spousal annuity trusts allow a married Medicaid applicant to convert excess assets (that would otherwise disqualify him or her from Medicaid) into a lifetime income for the community spouse. A spousal annuity trust allows a Medicaid applicant with excess assets to become immediately eligible for Medicaid. A transfer to a spousal annuity trust works for two reasons: first, the transfer is not a disqualifying transfer if the trust meets the requirements set out below, *and,* second, distributions from the trust to the community spouse are not counted as the applicant's assets as long as distributions under the trust commence *after* the Medicaid application is approved. A transfer to a spousal annuity trust is *not* treated as a divestment under Medicaid *if* the following conditions are met:

- The trust is irrevocable;
- Other than trustee fees, all trust income and principal must be used for the community spouse; and
- The trust must make distributions at least annually to the community spouse that are actuarially calculated to use up all trust assets during the spouse's lifetime using life expectancy tables provided in the regulations. Note that distributions in excess of the required minimum annual distribution are permitted.

A spousal annuity trust may be created even after you have entered the nursing home. Timing is important: the trust should be funded *after* the snapshot date (to get the greatest CSRA), and *before* the Medicaid application is filed (so the assets are not counted). The community spouse typically creates the trust for her own benefit using countable assets (of any kind including liquid assets, real estate, notes receivable, etc.). To preserve the integrity of the trust, it is advisable that neither the community spouse nor the applicant act as trustee. Assets remaining in the trust on the death of the community spouse, if any, are distributed to the beneficiaries named in the trust or to the revocable trust of the community spouse.

Half a Loaf

As noted above, the length of disqualification for transfers during the look back period is calculated by dividing the amount transferred by the average cost of private pay nursing home care in Michigan. The fact that the disqualification period is based on the monthly cost of nursing home care creates an interesting mathematical phenomenon: if you give away half of your countable assets, the half you keep will sustain you in the nursing home for a period equal to the disqualification period. For example, Adam Baum, a widower, has $100,000 in a money market and no other assets. He knows he will have to enter a nursing home in the near future and would like to preserve as much of his $100,000 for his family as possible. If he does nothing, he will enter the nursing home and privately pay until his $100,000 is reduced to $2,000, at which time Medicaid will take over. If, instead, he gives $50,000 to his children (creating a nine-month disqualification period), he will have the remaining $50,000 to cover his nursing home costs during that time. The net effect is that Adam preserved $50,000 for his family that otherwise would have been lost.

Adam's example is a little simplistic. Actually, Adam's patient pay amount –which is derived from his monthly income –

would offset a portion of his cost allowing him to gift *more* than half the loaf.

Serial divestment and spousal annuity trusts result in virtually no disqualification period, and are therefore preferred over the half a loaf technique (with its roughly fifty percent disqualification period). The half a loaf technique is rarely used in Michigan since serial divestment will always produce a better result. However, the half a loaf tool may become useful in the future if Michigan's serial divestment rules change.

Annuities

Excess countable assets can be converted to income through the purchase of an *actuarially sound* annuity. To be actuarially sound, the annuity cannot be guaranteed to extend beyond the life expectancy of the applicant. The purchase of the annuity is not a divestment because it is a transfer for value. By converting countable assets to income, you become immediately eligible for Medicaid. Despite the fact that the income payments from the annuity are counted as part of the patient pay amount, substantial savings result by immediately removing the entire purchase price of the annuity from the applicant's countable assets. Purchase of an annuity is a planning tool of last resort to be used when you have already entered the nursing home and cannot use the spousal annuity trust (if you're not married), serial divestment (which may take several months to implement), or other techniques that involve advance planning. To minimize the impact of annuity income on the patient pay amount annuities were often structured to pay a minimal amount of income up to the date of the applicant's life expectancy. If the applicant survived, the balance of the annuity value would be distributed in a balloon payment shortly before the end of the applicant's life expectancy (giving rise to the term *balloon annuity*). The use of annuities in Medicaid planning is likely to be limited as a result of action by the Michigan Department of Community Health. Effective June 1,

2005, the purchase of an annuity is treated as a divestment unless annuity payments are made in equal installments and the State of Michigan is named as the beneficiary of any amounts of remaining on the applicant's death.

Retirement Accounts

Retirement accounts, such as IRAs and 401(k)s present special planning problems. Retirement accounts – which can constitute a substantial percentage of your assets – are considered countable assets even when owned by a community spouse. Added complications when dealing with retirement accounts include the fact that distributions are subject to income tax, and that the *required minimum distribution* rules of the Internal Revenue Code must be met if you are age 70 1/2 or older. All of these factors must be taken into consideration when retirement accounts are involved.

One solution is to simply liquidate a portion or all of the retirement account, pay the income tax on the withdrawal, and then use the techniques discussed in this Chapter Six, such as serial divestment, to become Medicaid eligible. Naturally, there would be a substantial income tax liability that would have to be weighed against the potential Medicaid savings. The tax consequences of the distribution could be softened if you qualify for special *ten year averaging* on the distribution. You would also be eligible to offset some of the tax liability by deducting your private pay amount.

Another solution is to roll the retirement account into an irrevocable qualified annuity that meets both the income tax and Medicaid minimum distribution requirements. Michigan's proposed annuity policy, discussed above, reduces the desirability of this option since it requires that the State of Michigan be named as the beneficiary of the annuity upon your death. This approach could still be viable, however, for smaller retirement accounts that could be distributed in a relatively short period of time, and where you are married and the distributions are paid directly to your spouse (and therefore not added to your patient pay amount).

Still another solution is to initiate an irrevocable distribution scheme directly from the retirement account that meets both minimum distribution requirements. This, in effect, turns the retirement account into an annuity. It is not clear if and how Michigan's proposed annuity policy would affect this technique.

Medicaid Application

The Michigan Department of Human Services (DHS), formerly known as the Family Independence Agency (FIA), formerly known as the Department of Social Services, administers the Medicaid program in Michigan. DHS offices in your area can be located on the DHS Web site: www.mfia.state.mi.us. Form FIA 4572 is used to make application for nursing home benefits, and form FIA 1171 is the appropriate form when making application to the MI Choice program. If you are married, Asset Declaration form FIA-4574B must also be filed (containing financial information as of the snapshot date). A copy of Form FIA-4574B is reproduced at the end of Chapter Five. Forms are available at any local DHS office and are now available online. All forms require detailed financial information as well as supporting documentation to verify each financial entry. Your spouse, family member or guardian may sign your application if you are unable to do so. If someone other than you signs the application he is referred to as your *authorized representative*. If you qualify, Medicaid benefits begin on the first day of the month in which the application is filed. If it is coming to the end of the month, you should submit your application – even if you haven't supplied all of the supporting documentation – to preserve benefits for that month. You may submit the information when later requested by the DHS office. You will not prejudice your application if you supply the information within the requested time frame (you may even be able to get an extension). You may also apply for retroactive Medicaid benefits for the three months prior to the month of filing if you submit a Retroactive Medicaid Application form FIA-3243. The DHS has 45 days from the date of your filing to either grant or deny Medicaid benefits.

Annual Reporting

You must continue to meet Medicaid's medical and financial eligibility requirements after your initial qualification. There is much to do after initial qualification:

- You are required to immediately report any changes that would affect your eligibility such as receipt of an inheritance or the sale of an exempt asset (which as a result of the sale would become countable);
- You must disclose and verify your assets annually on form FIA-4574. Note that you are not required to disclose the assets of your community spouse, if any, after initial qualification; and
- Your assets may not exceed $2,000 in any month.

Follow Up for Married Applicants

To avoid inadvertent disqualification, the community spouse must do the following after the applicant spouse's Medicaid application is approved:

- The community spouse has one year (starting the first day after the Medicaid application is filed) to physically transfer her community spouse resource allowance into her sole name. If the CSRA is not moved before the end of the one-year period (called the *presumed asset eligibility period*) it will be counted as part of the institutionalized spouse's assets causing disqualification;
- Exempt assets should also be transferred to the community spouse. Although the one year presumed asset eligibility period does not apply to exempt assets, all exempt assets should be transferred to the community spouse as soon as

possible. Moving exempt assets to the community spouse accomplishes two objectives: first, the competent community spouse is better able to manage the assets; and second, it allows for the sale of the exempt assets without disqualifying the institutionalized spouse. Assets in the sole name of the community spouse, whether counted or exempt, are not considered to be available to the nursing home spouse. Therefore, if the community spouse wishes to dispose of an exempt asset (let's say the home), she can do so without disqualifying the institutionalized spouse;

- Any joint trust created by the couple for estate planning purposes must be revoked during the presumed asset eligibility period; otherwise the entire trust will be considered to be available to the nursing home spouse;
- The community spouse must *disinherit* the nursing home spouse. It is not uncommon for the community spouse to predecease the nursing home spouse. If the community spouse leaves his or her assets to the nursing home spouse, the inheritance would cause disqualification. If the community spouse would like to make assets available to the nursing home spouse at death, a testamentary special needs trust may be used for this purpose. Testamentary trusts (those created by Will) are not counted as owned by the institutionalized spouse;
- The community spouse may wish to do her own Medicaid planning using the techniques described above; and
- The spousal income allowance, if applicable, must be removed monthly from the institutionalized spouse's account to avoid have the nursing home spouse accumulate assets in excess of $2,000.

The three fact patterns on the pages that follow illustrate the planning techniques and strategies described in this Chapter Six.

FACT PATTERN ONE

FACTS:

Igor Beaver is an elderly widower with three adult children. He owns the following assets:

1. A home $150,000
   (with a mortgage of $35,000)
2. Bank Accounts $ 50,000
3. Brokerage Account $ 75,000
4. Automobile $ 15,000

His monthly income includes Social Security in the amount of $850 and a pension of $1,200. He has a proper Medicaid durable power of attorney.

What can be done to qualify Igor for Medicaid?

Igor Beaver has total assets of $290,000 with a net worth of $255,000 ($290,000 less mortgage of $35,000). The home and automobile are not countable, so he has $125,000 of countable assets. That is $123,000 "too much" to qualify for Medicaid. We have to deal with the $123,000.

1. **Convert Countable Assets to Non-Countable.** Take some cash out of the bank and pay off the mortgage. That will reduce the countable assets by $35,000, with no decrease in net worth. He could also buy a more expensive house. Or, he could fix up the house by putting on a new roof, new carpet, etc.
2. **Outright Gifts.** Igor could gift $88,000 (123,000-35,000) to his children resulting in 16 months ($88,000/5,367=16.39=16) of ineligibility due to divestment.
3. **Half-a-loaf.** He could gift $44,000 to his children. That would result in eight months of ineligibility. During those eight months he can use the ungifted $44,000 to pay for the nursing home. (Simplified example-actual calculation

takes into account income)

*4. **Purchase Annuity.** He could use the $88,000 to buy an annuity. Purchase of the annuity would not be a divestment as long as the annuity will not be guaranteed to pay out longer than his life expectancy. However, the income from the annuity will go toward the nursing home expense, **and** if he exceeds his life expectancy, there is no value left in the annuity contract for his heirs.

*5. **Purchase Balloon Annuity.** He could purchase a balloon annuity with the $88,000. The annuity would pay about $88 per month, which may go to the nursing home. One month short of his life expectancy, the annuity will pay about $87, 982.

6. **Serial Divestment-simple.** Gift $5,367, or less, per month. 5,366/5,367=.99. Round down=0 months of divestment penalty. Each month is a new gifting period. This will take 16 months to get rid of the $88,000.

7. **Serial Divestment-fancy.** Gift $10,499 *per month.* The divestment penalty is 1.99, or rounded down, 1. The ineligibility will be for the month of the gift, only. Do the same thing the next month and so on. This will use up the excess assets in less than eight months.

Note that these techniques could even be applied once Igor Beaver enters the nursing home, but before the Medicaid application is filed. The sooner they are started, however, the sooner he can obtain eligibility and the more options there are.

 * *Note that the annuity strategies (4 and 5) may be inadvisable after June 1, 2005 in light of proposed Medicaid eligibility policy changes issued by the Michigan Department of Community Health.*

FACT PATTERN TWO

FACTS:
Herb L. Remmedy and his wife, Anita, are an elderly couple with three adult children. Between the two of them, they own the following assets:

1. Home	$175,000
2. Financial Accounts	$250,000
3. Automobile	$ 15,000

Her monthly income is Social Security of $850 and a pension of $300. His monthly income is Social Security of $1,100 and pension of $1,000

What can be done to qualify Mr. Remmedy for Medicaid?

Mr. and Mrs. Remmedy have total assets of $440,000. The home and automobile are not countable, so there are $250,000 worth of countable assets.

1. **Community Spouse Resource Allowance.** Anita gets to keep 1/2 of the countable assets, up to $95,160. One-half of $250,000 is $125,000. She gets $95,160. That leaves $154,840 in assets, or $152,840 "too much".
2. **Gifts.** Use any of the gifting techniques discussed in Fact Pattern One.
*3. **Purchase Annuity.** Use the $152,840 to buy an annuity. So long as the annuity will not be guaranteed to pay out longer than Mrs. Remmedy's life expectancy, it will not be a divestment. However, if she outlives her life expectancy, there is no value left in the annuity contract for her heirs.
4. **Spousal Annuity Trust.** Place the excess $152,840 in a trust "solely for the benefit of "Mrs. Remmedy." The trust must be scheduled to pay out to her the entire balance of the trust within her life expectancy, *or shorter.* As the assets are paid out to her she can use them as she wishes. Her assets

will no longer count against Mr. Remmedy's eligibility, once he qualifies.

Note that these techniques could even be applied after Mr. Remmedy enters the nursing home, but before the Medicaid application is filed. The annuity strategy may not be available after June 1, 2005.

* *Note that the annuity strategy may be inadvisable after June 1, 2005 in light of proposed Medicaid eligibility policy changes issued by the Michigan Department of Community Health.*

FACT PATTERN THREE

FACTS:

Joe King and Mae King are an elderly couple with three adult children. Between the two of them, they own the following assets:

1. Home	$175,000
2. Financial Accounts	$ 90,000
3. Automobile	$ 15,000

Her monthly income is Social Security of $850 and a pension of $300. His monthly income is Social Security of $1,100 and pension of $1,000

What can be done to qualify Mr. King for Medicaid?

Mr. and Mrs. King have total assets of $280,000. The home and automobile are not countable, so there are $90,000 of countable assets.

1. **Community Spouse Resource Allowance.** Mrs. King gets to keep 1/2 of the countable assets, up to $95,160. One-half of $90,000 is $45,000. That leaves $45,000 in assets, or $43,000 "too much".
2. **Make House a Countable Asset.** *Before* Mr. King enters the nursing home, place the home into a revocable living trust. That makes the house a countable asset bringing the total value of the countable assets to $265,000 as of the date Mr. King enters the nursing home; the "snapshot date". The assets on the snapshot date are used to figure the Community Spouse Resource Allowance. One half of $265,000 is more than $95,160, so Mrs. King gets to keep $95,160. Then *before* the Medicaid application is filed, remove the house from the trust and place it in Mrs. King's name. All of the countable assets are less than the $95,160 CSRA on the application date and therefore Mr. King is

immediately eligible for Medicaid. No Joe King. There is a critical difference between the snapshot date and the application date that allows this to work.

3. **Spousal Annuity Trust.** If there were any assets in excess of the CSRA, place into a Spousal Annuity Trust.

Chapter Seven

The Future

The aging of our population coupled with current federal and state budget deficits portends trouble in the coming decades. In 2002, roughly 12.4 percent of Michigan's population was age 65 or older. By 2020, that number is expected to go to 16.9 percent, representing a *36 percent increase*. Clearly, government continues to carry the bulk of the load when it comes to paying for long term care. Medicaid covers two-thirds of all nursing home residents. For the immediate future, Michigan, like most states, is facing fiscal problems of unprecedented proportions. Until revenues recover, states will be forced to consider cuts in every area including Medicaid spending. Increasingly, long term care will be scrutinized for budget savings. Unless there is meaningful fiscal relief at the federal level, states will be unable to sustain the fiscal burden of Medicaid in the long run, and budget driven program reductions can be expected to continue.

State Reaction

Between 2002 and 2004 at least 19 states implemented programs to reduce long term care spending. Basically, the programs were aimed at lowering reimbursement levels for nursing homes and tightening eligibility and funding for home and community based services. These changes no doubt made access to care more difficult in these states, and threaten the quality of care. Other states have taken a more aggressive approach to limit or prevent the asset transfer techniques described in Chapter Six, and have implemented estate asset recovery. As noted, Michigan recently enacted new medical eligibility standards in an attempt to reduce the number of citizens eligible to enter the nursing home at government expense.

Budget cutbacks directly impact the availability and quality of care. To be assured of receiving quality care, consumers will need to educate themselves as to their options and rights. The educated consumer will be much more likely to find quality care and scarce government subsidies. Unless there are dramatic changes in the long term delivery system in the U.S., uninformed consumers will face long waiting lists and receive substandard care.

Estate Recovery

Since 1993, Federal law has required Michigan to seek reimbursement of its Medicaid expenditures from the *estate* of deceased recipients. The amount the state is required to recover is the full cost of Medicaid-provided nursing home care, MI Choice expenditures, hospital care and prescription drugs. Each state is free to define *estate* as it sees fit. Some states limit the definition to the decedent's probate estate while others have adopted a broader definition that includes all assets of the decedent, including jointly held property and property owned in trust.

Despite the federal mandate, Michigan is the *only state in the country* that has not implemented an estate recovery program. To date, no Michigan legislator has wanted to pass legislation to confiscate grandma's house. It seems, however, that political and budgetary pressure is mounting to implement some form of estate recovery in the near future. The exact form of the legislation – how it will define estate, and whether the state will use liens to secure the Medicaid recipient's obligation – is unclear. Once passed, informed families will no doubt structure their assets to minimize the impact of estate recovery.

Estate recovery has proven to be an extremely poor source of revenue for those states that have implemented estate recovery programs. The national average for estate recovery is less than one tenth of one percent of total Medicaid expenditures. Certainly, estate recovery will not cure the current Medicaid crisis in this country.

Needless to say, the rules and planning techniques described in Chapter Six are subject to change. Although unlikely, some of the changes could be made retroactively, affecting planning already in place. You should seek qualified professional help from an elder law attorney when you engage in any form of Medicaid planning, and review that planning regularly. You should also seek help when making application for Medicaid to ensure that your application is accurate and correct. False information can result in Medicaid disqualification or even criminal penalties.

Move to More In-Home and Community Based Care

One solution is for states to overcome the institutional bias and focus on in-home and community based care. States like Oregon, Washington, Colorado, Vermont and Arizona have demonstrated that they can stretch their Medicaid dollar by providing greater access to home and community-based care. Nationally, Medicaid spending on nursing homes per capita was $154 in 2003 as compared to $95 for home and community-based services. Nonetheless, approximately two-thirds (67%) of Medicaid long-term care funds go toward institutional care. The trend toward in-home and community care was strong in the early 1990s until –for budgetary reasons – it stalled in 1997. Spending on in-home and community based care grew at a 31 percent average annual rate between 1990 and 1997, and then slowed to a 15 percent annual rate of growth after 1997. In-home and community based care appears to hold great promise as a way of holding down long term care costs and is universally preferred by seniors. Strong family support is required to supplement in-home care since in-home care is not available on an around-the-clock basis. You should consider long term care insurance if you do not have a strong family structure or for whatever reason your family is not able to provide for your care.

The Nursing Home Industry

Nursing homes aren't immune from government cutbacks and the increasing focus on in-home care. Nursing homes have felt the pinch as seniors have elected to receive in-home care, and the gap between private pay and Medicaid reimbursement has grown. The number of nursing home residents (down 5.7%), beds (down 4.6%), and occupancy rates have all declined across the country the last five years. The average occupancy rate in Michigan nursing homes is 84.4%, ranking us 28th in the country. During this same period, in-home and community based care has increased significantly. Thus, it's not surprising that hospital discharge planners and nursing home operators try to cherry pick private pay and Medicare residents (while wait-listing Medicaid applicants); their survival may very well depend on it.

Be Proactive

The growing senior population coupled with historic government budget deficits has put a strain on the long term care delivery system with no relief in sight. Although a shift to in-home and community based care, and the other cost cutting measures contemplated by the states may relieve some pressure, the system faces significant challenges in the future. Ironically, when a similar analysis of the Social Security system is presented to the public, we have universally concluded that it is foolish to rely on the Social Security system as our primary source of retirement income. Yet, when it comes to planning for care in our twilight years, we naively cling to the belief that the government will take care of us. We recommend the following course of action to ensure that you get good care:

- Educate yourself. Understanding the system will allow you to obtain the best care and take full advantage of the government programs designed for your benefit;
- Prepare advance directives such as those discussed in Chapter One to allow your family or friends to advocate on your behalf in the event that you are unable to make your own decisions;
- Plan ahead. Many programs, such as subsidized senior housing and MI Choice, have waiting lists. Advance planning will enhance your chances of aging in place. It is much more likely that you can stay in your own home if you use the care management provided by AAA or a private geriatric care manager;
- Make yourself Medicaid eligible – using the techniques described in Chapter Six – to preserve as much of your assets as possible for your supplemental care (care not provided by Medicaid like specialized medical and dental care) and to leave a legacy to your heirs; and.
- Investigate long term care insurance. Insuring against the risk of needing long term care, and having dollars earmarked for your care, will increase the likelihood that you will be able to stay in your home or gain entry into a quality nursing home as *you* so determine.

Notes

Chapter Eight

Long Term Care Insurance

James M. Knaus, CFP®

Most people say they don't want to be a burden on anyone, especially their children. Clients are worried about running out of money in retirement, and the potential cost of an extended nursing home stay terrifies them. It's not only the skilled nursing home costs that are worrisome, but also assisted living and home health care. In fact, it has become increasingly clear that people want to remain in their own homes while receiving needed care. If around-the-clock care is needed for home health care, the costs will exceed those of skilled nursing home care.

The first and most important concern of most families is high quality care. Those who can afford to private pay for a nursing home will qualify for the best facilities. At the other end of the spectrum are those who, due to minimal resources, are limited to facilities that accept Medicaid for at least a certain number of the available beds. Some patients pay their own way until they have spent down their assets sufficiently to qualify for Medicaid.

Beyond not wanting to be a burden on their children, many prefer to preserve enough of their assets to leave an inheritance. The three principal methods to accomplish this goal are:

- Medicaid qualifying techniques described in Chapter Six
- Self-insurance
- Long Term Care (LTC) insurance

Self-insurance is a concept known as *risk retention* whereby the individual or couple has sufficient assets and/or cash flow to handle long term care expenses privately. People often ask: "How much is enough?"

Let's start with an example of a single person. Anita Knapp has Social Security benefits of $1,400 per month plus a pension from her deceased husband of $1,600 per month. Moreover, financial assets (stocks, bonds, mutual funds, retirement accounts) total $300,000. Assuming a 5% current yield on the investments, an additional $15,000 per year, or $1,250 per month can be generated.

Note that a 5% current yield is not necessarily a sustainable current yield (dividends and interest). With a mix of equity and fixed income securities, the hope is that growth of the principal will allow a growing income stream to offset inflation.

Cash Flow Source	Monthly Amount
Social Security	$1,400
Pension	$1,600
Investment Income	$1,250
Total	$4,250/month = $51,000 per year

Since the cost for nursing home care (and other expenses) exceed $51,000 per year (the average cost in Michigan in 2005 is $64,404), Anita will be dipping into principal. Anita is a candidate for some amount of long term care insurance since her income does not cover the cost of her nursing home care.

The ability to self-insure is even more problematic for a couple, because the expense level of the community spouse may decrease only slightly. Our next example on the following page, then, is a couple, Ben and Anna Splitt, with their financial information.

While this cash flow is enough to handle the long term care costs of one of the spouses, the question remains whether the community spouse has sufficient cash flow to maintain the household and herself.

Cash Flow Source	Monthly Amount
Social Security: Ben	$1,800
Social Security: Anna	$900
Pension	$3,000
Assets: $600,000 Current Yield: 5%	$2,500
Total	$8,200/month = $98,400 per year

The message is that long term care financial planning is required to project various scenarios under different assumptions. You may or may not be *able* to self insure the long term care risk. The examples of Anita Knapp and Ben & Anna Splitt were intended to show situations that could go either way.

That's where LTC insurance planning comes into play. The catch is that you must be healthy enough at the time of application to qualify for coverage. But if you're healthy, you may not feel the need. If you're *not* healthy, you certainly want the coverage, but you won't qualify.

So let's cut to the chase. If you're healthy – and relatively young – you must consider the risk of a long term care obligation and the opportunity to transfer the risk to an insurance company. You may consciously decide to self-insure the risk if you have sufficient assets. Or, you might have unwittingly self-insured by doing nothing.

Our advice is for you to make a conscious decision after assessing your own objectives, resources, and limitations.

What to Look For in a Policy

Assuming you're in a position to consider long term care insurance, what elements are most important? Listed below are policy benefits and features most advisors recommend.

- Adequate Monthly (or Daily) Benefit
- Sufficient Length of Coverage (Number of Years)

- Reasonable Waiting Period (Elimination Period)
- Suitable Inflation Protection
- Guaranteed Renewability
- Waiver of Premium Benefit
- Coverage for
  - Skilled Nursing Care
  - Assisted Living
  - Home Health Care
- Favorable Tax Treatment

These are the core benefits of any LTC policy. If you specify the criteria you want in a policy, comparison-shopping is significantly easier because policies are essentially standardized.

Many other features are available if they fit with your needs. For example:

- Waiver of Elimination Period for Home Health Care
- Enhanced Return of Premium Feature
- Non-Forfeiture Provision
- Shared Care Riders
- Family Care Benefits
- Survivorship and Waiver Benefits
- Additional Cash Benefits

Most of these features are nice to have but not mandatory. They will add substantially to the cost, so be selective.

With all these provisions to consider, we'll need to define some terms. In fact, you may want to see a specimen policy. Please refer to a reasonably representative sample policy available through the Web site www.jhancock.com.[1]

---

[1] This is not meant to be a recommendation of any specific policy or company. Please consult with a properly licensed professional who specializes in LTC insurance.

Definitions and Explanations
Adequate Monthly Benefit

Notice that we refer to the monthly benefit. We prefer the monthly benefit approach to the daily benefit approach, because the maximum monthly benefit covers all eligible expenses during the month, whereas the daily approach would require a daily qualification for benefits and a daily limit. Let's use an example of the difference between a policy with a $4,500/month benefit and another policy with a daily benefit of $150.

Service	Dates or Cost	Monthly Approach $4,500/month	Daily Approach $150/day
Skilled Care $300/day	5 Days	Full Benefit $1,500	Subject to Daily Limit: $750
Assisted Living $100/day	25 days	Full Benefit $2,500	Full Benefit $2,500
Occupational and Speech Therapy	$400 during Assisted Living	Full Benefit $400	Full Benefit $400
TOTAL		$4,400	$3,650

The monthly benefit approach, in essence, provides a pool of dollars that can be used for any combination of eligible services without a *daily* limit. Remember that the maximum benefit period (below) also provides an *aggregate* pool of dollars under the policy.

→ Advice: Purchase benefits based on a maximum *monthly benefit*.
→ Advice: Make sure home health care coverage is at least 80% or 100% of the skilled nursing home benefit.

Benefit Period and Policy Limit

The maximum *benefit period* is the number of years for which benefits are payable. The most common choices are:

- Two Years
- Three Years
- Four Years
- Five Years
- Six Years
- Ten Years
- Unlimited Benefits

The *policy limit* is determined by multiplying the monthly benefit amount by the benefit period. For example:

$3,000/month *times* 4 years [48 months] = $144,000 Policy Limit

The policy limit, then, can also be viewed as a pool of dollars available during the lifetime of the policyholder. Note: The policy limit may be increased due to inflation adjustments (see below).

Ideally, the policyholder would prefer unlimited benefits, but the premium may be excessively high and beyond budgetary constraints. As a result, clients will compromise and select a benefit period that is not only affordable but provides reasonable coverage for the most likely scenario. The average length of stay in a nursing facility is just under two years, and the look back period for transfers is three years. The natural inclination, then, is to select a three-year benefit period. Unfortunately, the client might be on the wrong side of the average and run out of coverage.

In designing a long term care policy, the client, with the help of the professional, will reach a point where the premium is still affordable and the mix of benefits is suitable to transfer an optimal amount of risk to the insurance company. Beyond that bucket of benefits, the client is self-insured. Personal assets must be used from that point forward, or other resources must be located for funding, such as Medicaid. Although the strategy of combining insurance with anticipated eligibility for Medicaid may make sense now, the rules for Medicaid are subject to change due to possible funding cuts as the population ages.

Elimination Period (Waiting Period)

The elimination period is the number of days for which no benefits are payable. In other words, the elimination period is the waiting period before benefits kick in.

The most liberal provision for the waiting period lets you satisfy the requirement only once during the life of the policy, using dates of service that need not be consecutive and qualifying for eligibility in multiple ways. In some well-designed policies, if you receive home health care for one or more days in a calendar week, the company will apply *seven* days toward the satisfaction of the elimination period.

The longer the elimination period, the lower the premium. The most common choices of elimination period are: 30, 60, 90, 180, and 365 days. Most clients can self-insure the short-term risks and will gravitate toward the 90-day waiting period as an optimal cost/benefit mix.

→ Advice: Generally select the 90-day elimination period.

Inflation Protection

The cost of long term care services has risen more steeply than the general cost of living. A policy without inflation protection will become inadequate in a relatively short time frame. Consequently, most advisors recommend a cost of living adjustment in one form or another. Common alternatives include:

- 5% simple inflation (5% increase in the benefits each year, based on the *original* benefit amount)
- 5% compound inflation (5% increase in benefits each year, based on the *prior* year's benefit amount)
- 5%/3% (5% compound inflation adjustment on the monthly [or daily] benefit amount, but with a 3% compound inflation adjustment maximum on the policy limit).

The compound inflation protection approach is, of course, the most expensive. For example, observe the difference in the twentieth year:

Original Benefit	5% Simple over 20 Years	5% Compound over 20 Years
$4,000/month	$8,000/month	$10,613/month

Many advisors advocate the compound approach, but my experience is that the premium commitment is so relatively high that clients will select the simple inflation approach, knowing that they are self-insuring an increasing proportion of the cost.

→ Advice: Consider your ability to handle the compound inflation approach, but if the premiums are too steep, use the simple inflation approach.

Guaranteed Renewable

Virtually all policies sold are guaranteed renewable, which means that the insurance company guarantees to continue (renew) the policy each year as long as the policyholder pays the premium, but reserves the right to increase premiums on a class basis. For example, the company can increase the premiums for all LTC policies of a particular form in Michigan by a certain percentage. However, an exorbitant premium increase may cause an indirect form of adverse selection that would negatively affect the insurance company: healthy people drop the coverage while the least healthy maintain it. Adverse selection will exacerbate the problem for the insurance company, and its claims experience will continue to worsen. Thus, insurance companies will tend to price the product carefully in the first place to avoid the necessity of increasing premiums later.

An extreme example of proper pricing is a non-cancellable policy, in which the policy is guaranteed renewable at the *original* premium. A non-can policy is exceedingly difficult to find and would be very expensive.

Waiver of Premium

The waiver of premium benefit means that the policyholder is relieved of premium paying responsibility (after a waiting period) while receiving LTC benefits. The waiting period for waiver of premium is generally the same as the policy's elimination period. If the elimination period has been satisfied, and benefits are payable (for most eligible services), premiums will be waived. If and when benefits are no longer payable, the policyholder must resume premium payments.

Major Covered Services

Most policies contain broad definitions of the services covered. The most important are:

- Skilled Nursing Care
- Assisted Living
- Adult Day Care
- Home Health Care

Regardless of the location, benefits are payable if the insured person:

- Needs assistance with two or more *Activities of Daily Living* (ADLs) namely bathing, continence, dressing, eating, toileting, and transferring.
- Needs continual supervision due to a cognitive impairment in order to protect the insured from threats to health and safety.

Certain logical exclusions and limitations are common in all policies, such as intentionally self-inflicted injury, alcoholism and drug addiction.

→ Advice: Make sure your policy covers you where you want to be treated. If you need coverage outside the U.S. and Canada, you should inquire about international coverage.

Tax Qualified

Virtually all LTC policies sold now are tax qualified, meaning that federal tax law allows for favorable results as follows:

- Premiums paid by individual taxpayers are eligible (within limits, listed below) as a medical expense itemized deduction.
- Benefits received (again, within limits) are income tax free.

A number of rules must be satisfied in order to qualify for these tax benefits.

→ The services required by a *chronically ill* individual must be provided under a treatment plan prescribed by a licensed health care practitioner.
→ A chronically ill individual is one who is unable to perform at least two of the activities of daily living for at least 90 days, or who requires protective supervision because of severe cognitive impairment.

Current law limits the annual amount of LTC premiums that are eligible for a tax deduction, based on the age of the insured. The amounts are adjusted annually for inflation.

Age Before Close of Tax Year	2005 Limitation
40 or Less	$270
41 to 50	$510
51 to 60	$1,020
61 to 70	$2,720
Over 70	$3,400

As to the medical expense deduction, individuals or couples who itemize can deduct unreimbursed medical expenses and health insurance premiums (including LTC premiums) to the extent of the excess over 7.5% of adjusted gross income (AGI).

For example, let's assume the situation of Jerry Attrick, age 67, a widower. His AGI is $40,000, while his unreimbursed medical expenses are $2,000. He also pays $2,800 per year for LTC and $938.40 per year for his Medicare Part B ($78.20/month withheld from his Social Security check).

Jerry Attrick's Example

Item	Amount
Adjusted Gross Income	$40,000
Times 7.5% (Threshold)	$3,000
Calculation	
Unreimbursed Medical Expenses	$2,000
LTC Premium (Limited in 2005)	+$2,720
Medicare Part B Premium	+$938
Total Eligible Expenses	$5,658
Less Threshold of $3,000	**Itemized Deduction $2,658**

If you don't itemize, under current law you get no federal income tax deduction for unreimbursed medical expenses and health insurance premiums. In Jerry Attrick's case, his total itemized deductions must be more than $5,000 before he obtains an advantage from itemizing. Even if his home is free and clear, his totals might look like this:

Medical Expenses over the Threshold:	$2,658
Mortgage Interest	0
Real Estate Tax	$3,000
State Income Tax	$1,600
Charitable Contributions	$1,200
Total Itemized Deductions	**$8,458**

In this case, Jerry gets a benefit from itemizing this year because the itemized deductions exceed the standard deduction of $5,000.

If Jerry were married, the standard deduction for a married couple filing a joint return in 2005 is $10,000. As a result, with the same itemized deductions as shown above, the married couple would take the higher standard deduction.

In either case, the benefits from a long term care policy will still be income tax free, up to $4,500 per month in 2005.

Special Tax Situations
Self-Employed Taxpayers

Self-employed business owners (sole proprietors and partners as well as members in Limited Liability Companies and S Corporation Shareholders) are able to deduct LTC premiums in full (subject to the limits above) as an adjustment to income on page one of Form 1040. In other words, the deduction is available to them whether or not they itemize.

Corporate Taxpayers

Corporate employers can pay LTC premiums on behalf of employees (and can discriminate) and take a corporate income tax deduction. The premium paid is not taxable to the employee. Benefits are income tax free.

For employer-sponsored group LTC plans, certain advantages may be evident:

- More liberal underwriting
- Ability to insure parents more easily
- Steeper discounts
- Portability

Comment

As part of the effort to reform and simplify the federal tax system, some commentators have suggested that individual taxpayers should have the same page one deduction as an adjustment to income enjoyed by self-employed taxpayers. The improved access to the deduction would likely increase LTC purchases substantially.

Additional Benefits

Additional benefits may be payable under a *stay-at-home* provision that facilitates the ability to receive LTC services in the home. These are specific benefits *in addition* to Home Health Care benefits. Examples include:

- Home modifications (ramps, shower bars, wider doorways, etc.)
- Emergency Medical Response System
- Durable Medical Equipment (hospital-style bed, wheelchair)
- Caregiver Training (for uncompensated caregivers)
- Home Safety Check (to make sure the home is adequately *senior-proofed*)
- Provider Care Check (to ensure that providers are competent)

With the burgeoning population of older persons, and the limited number of nursing facilities, the stay-at-home option will become increasingly popular and is automatically included in some policies.

→ Advice: Select a policy with liberal and broad features that allow qualification for benefits in multiple ways.

Core Benefit Comparisons

In view of the standardization of LTC policies mentioned above, it's easier to do comparison-shopping, but not foolproof. You could invite a parade of agents to make their recommendations, after which you can assemble a spreadsheet showing benefits and costs. Another alternative is to ask an independent specialist to do the comparison-shopping for you. In either case, the spreadsheet might look as shown on the following page.

As a consumer, concentrate on the steak, not the sizzle. Ethical, competent advisors will do the same.

Benefit/Feature	Company A	Company B	Company C	Company D
Skilled Care	$4,500/month			
Assisted Living	$4,500/month			
Adult Day Care	$4,500/month			
Home Health Care	$4,500/month			
Benefit Period	6 Years			
Elimination Period	90 Days			
Inflation Option	5% Compound			
Waiver of Premium	Yes (90 Days)			
Tax Qualified	Yes			
Guaranteed Renewable	Yes			
Annual Premium	$2,500/year			

The benefits in the spreadsheet can be expanded to include the ancillary features that may be important to you. Once you're satisfied with your selection of core benefits from a handful of competitive insurance companies, consider the sizzle. List those features that you'd *like* to have in your ideal policy and weigh the cost/benefit ratio.

Next is a chart that shows representative premium comparisons based on an individual's health, ranging from *Preferred to Standard to Class 1.*

Premium Chart: Guaranteed Renewable
Male Age 60

Benefit	Preferred	Standard	Class 1
$4,500/month • Skilled Care • Assisted Living • Home Health Care			
Benefit Period: 6 Year			
Elimination Period: 90 Days			
Inflation: 5% Compound			
Annual Premium	$2,754	$3,240	$4,050

Affordability may be an issue for many people. The chart shows premium levels for a solid package of benefits, varying only by health status, and lets you inspect the major (core) components. If you feel the premium commitment is too high, you can scale back in a number of ways. For example, you may reduce the monthly benefit amount, shorten the benefit period, extend the elimination period or use simple inflation instead of compound inflation. Some families decide that the children or other heirs can pay the premiums themselves.

Note the impact that health has on the premium. In fact, as noted earlier, your health may have deteriorated to the point where you do not qualify for coverage at all.

Let's assume that you qualify for coverage at standard rates. Perhaps you are somewhat overweight or you have a condition that causes the insurance company underwriter some concern, such as arthritis. If you know your rating class (standard), you can then do some scenario testing. Examine the chart on the following page to see the reductions you can achieve through various changes.

If you and a spouse or partner are applying at the same time, you'll probably see a discount of 25% to 30% for each person.

The Cost of Waiting

The longer you wait to buy long term care insurance, the higher the premium. You may even price yourself out of the market, or you might become uninsurable. Again our example shows solid coverage, but at different ages, using current rates for a single male.

Benefit Amount: $4,500/month
Benefit Period: 10 Years
Elimination Period: 30 Days
5%/5% Inflation

Age	60	65	70	75
Annual Premium	$4,730	$6,094	$8,871	$13,246

Premium Differentials: Standard Class
Male Age 60

Benefit Amount: $4,500/month	$3,000/month Proportionate Reduction	$2,250/month Proportionate Reduction	$2,000/month Proportionate Reduction
Benefit Period: 10 Years	6 Years: **15% to 18% Reduction From 10 Year Plan**	4 Years: **30% to 35% Reduction From 10 Year Plan**	2 Years: **45% to 50% Reduction From 10 Year Plan**
Elimination Period: 30 Days	60 Days: **c. 8% Reduction From 30 Day EP**	90 Days: **c. 17% Reduction From 30 Day EP**	180 Days: **c. 25% Reduction From 30 Day EP**
Inflation: 5% Compound on: • Monthly • Aggregate	5% Compound on: • Monthly 3% Compound on: • Aggregate **c. 17% Reduction From 5%/5%**	5% Simple **c. 18% to 22% Reduction From 5%/5%**	

→ Advice: With all the potentially moving parts, ask your advisor to generate the comparison matrixes that reflect your most likely scenarios.

Let's return to the definitions now, concentrating on terms that are not necessarily *core benefits*.

Waiver of Elimination Period for Home Health Care

The waiver of elimination period for home health care is reasonably straightforward, and provides that benefits can be paid without satisfaction of the elimination period for:

- Home Health Care
- *Hospice Care* (in the home, a nursing home or assisted living facility)
- Adult Day Care

You must still satisfy the elimination period before benefits are payable under the LTC benefit for confinement in a nursing home or assisted living facility.

→ Advice: Self-insure this risk, and be prepared to pay your own way during the elimination period.

Enhanced Return of Premium Feature upon Death

This provision attempts to answer the objection that premiums are wasted if there are no significant claims. That's like hoping your house burns down so you get value from all those premiums you paid.

Nonetheless, the enhanced return of premium feature upon death compares total premiums paid to all benefits received. Any excess premiums paid over benefits received will be paid to the beneficiary, and may be taxable if the insured policyholder had enjoyed a tax deduction during life.

→ Advice: Skip it. Use the savings to maintain or purchase legitimate life insurance.

Note: As a standard part of the policy, a return of premium upon death rider would provide a death benefit over benefits already paid for death before age 65.

Non-Forfeiture Provision

Under a common form of this optional benefit, if the policy has been in force for more than three years, and the policy subsequently lapses for non-payment of premium, the policy will remain in effect with no premiums required, but the policy limit will be equal to the aggregate premiums paid.

→ Advice: You can pass on this rider under the assumption that you had planned to pay premiums anyway.

Shared Care Rider

The shared care rider is intended to be attached to two policies, one each for a husband and wife (or two committed partners). In the event that the limits under one policy are
exhausted, benefits are continued based on the remaining limits in the partner's policy.

The shared care rider may be especially useful if it is anticipated that one of the spouses (or partners) is more likely to incur
long term care expenses.

→ Advice: Consider this benefit for inclusion in your and
your partner's policies.

Family Care Benefits

The family care benefit allows the policyholder to designate
up to three family members who can have access to policy benefits. The rider may be viable for someone who wants to insure
parents or children under the same policy. The provisions of
the policy can become rather complicated, but in the right circumstances, the arrangement can satisfy multiple needs.

→ Advice: Consider this rider if your circumstances warrant.

Survivorship and Waiver Benefits

This rider allows a policyholder to enjoy a paid-up policy in
the event of death of a spouse/partner, usually if all of the following conditions are met:

• No benefits were paid under either policy during the first
ten years.
• Both policies had been in force for ten full consecutive
years (other than under a non-forfeiture benefit), and
• On the spouse's/partner's death, the survivorship and
waiver benefit rider had been in force for at least ten years.

In a similar way, premiums will be *waived* if all the conditions above are satisfied and premiums are being waived on the spouse's/partner's policy.

→ Advice: In view of the onerous conditions, the rider has dubious merits. Avoid it.

Additional Cash Benefits

In another effort to encourage home health care, this rider will pay additional cash amounts for any purpose as long as home health care benefits are paid during at least one day in the month and you have not been in a nursing home or assisted living facility. You must also have satisfied the elimination period and the ADL and/or cognitive impairment requirement.

→ Advice: Don't sweat the small stuff. Skip it.

Riders, Riders...Everywhere

If you've checked out the specimen or an actual policy, you know there are more riders than we have covered. We'll use a table (following page) to summarize our opinion of each rider's usefulness.

Rider	Description	Add, Avoid, or Automatic
Restoration of Benefits	Policy limit is restored if insured is claim-free for 180+ days	Consider adding for shorter benefit periods
Double Coverage for Accident	Doubles the LTC Benefit if services are required due to accident before age 65	Avoid
Respite Care	Gives relief to uncompensated caregiver up to 21 days per year	Automatic
Extension of Benefits	Policy benefits continue after lapsation of policy while in nursing home	Automatic (usually)
International Coverage	Benefits outside US and Canada: Limited to one year	Automatic (usually)
Return of Premium upon Death	If insured dies before age 65, excess of premiums over benefits paid is returned to beneficiary	Automatic
Grace Period	65 Days (more liberal than customary 31 days in most health insurance)	Automatic
Guaranteed Purchase Option	Right to buy additional 5%, 10% or 15% of LTC benefit every three years	An alternative to inflation riders; may be solid option
Contingent Non-forfeiture Provision	If insurance company raises premium beyond limits, insured has a right to reduce benefits, or have policy limits reduced to premiums already paid	Automatic

Final Note

Remember that insurance companies are in business for a number of reasons. A mutual insurance company is owned by the policyholders, so there are no stockholders to satisfy. A stock insurance company is owned by stockholders, who must be rewarded for the risks they assume.

In either case (mutual or stock company) the insurance company is genuinely interested in paying all legitimate claims. Otherwise policyholders would be upset and the company's poor reputation would spread.

On the other hand, premiums must be adequate, and ineligible claims must be denied in order for the insurance company to survive, grow and prosper for the benefit of all constituents: policyholders, beneficiaries, company owners, employees and the community. Thus, it makes sense to investigate the claims paying history of the company in addition to the financial stability. Sources for this purpose include A. M. Best & Company, Standard & Poor's, and Weiss. Most professional insurance advisors will be pleased to provide the A. M. Best rating and other details regarding any proposed company.

→ Final Advice: Be careful out there!

Notes

APPENDIX A
Area Agencies on Aging (AAA)

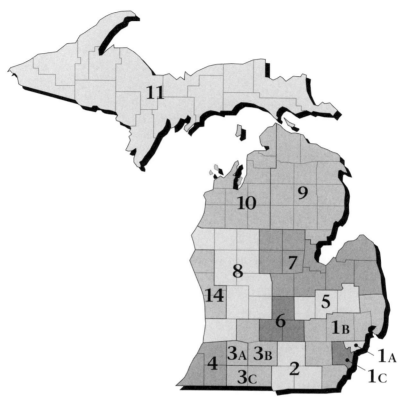

1-A Detroit Area Agency on Aging
Phone: (313) 446-4444
Serves: Cities of Detroit, Hamtramck,
Highland Park, all of the Grosse Pointes
and Harper Woods
www.daaala.org/daaa

1-B Area Agency on Aging
Phone: (248) 357-2255
Serves: Counties of Livingston, Macomb, Monroe, Oakland, St. Clair
and Washtenaw
www.aaalb.com

1-C The Senior Alliance – AAA
Phone: (734) 722-2830 or (800) 335-7881
Serves: All of Wayne County excluding those communities served by
Region 1-A

Region 2 Area - Agency on Aging
Phone: (517) 467-2204
Serves: Counties of Jackson, Hillsdale, Lenawee
www.r2aaa.org
Region 3-A - Area Agency on Aging
Phone: (269) 373-5200
Services: County of Kalamazoo

Region 3-B Area Agency on Aging
Phone: (269) 966-2450 or (800) 626-6719
Serves: Counties of Barry, Calhoun
Region 3-C Branch-St. Joseph Area Agency on Aging
Phone: (517) 279-8009 _ (888) 615-8009
Serves: Counties of Branch, St. Joseph

Region 4 Area Agency on Aging, Inc.
Phone: (269) 983-0177 or (800) 442-2803
Serves: Counties of Berrien, Cass, Van Buren
www.region-iv.org

Region 5 Valley Area Agency on Aging
Phone: (810) 239-7671 or (800) 978-6275
Serves: Counties of Genesee, Lapeer, Shiawassee
www.gfn.org/vaaa

Region 6 Tri County Office on Aging
Phone: (517) 887-1440 or (800) 405-9141
Serves: Counties of Clinton, Eaton, Ingham

Region 7 Area Agency on Aging
Phone: (989) 893-4506 or (800) 858-1637
Serves: Counties of Bay, Clare, Gladwin, Gratiot, Huron, Isabella,
Midland, Saginaw, Sanilac, Tuscola
www.region7aaa.org

Region 8 Area Agency on Aging of Western Michigan, Inc.
Phone: (616) 456-5664 or (888) 456-5664
Serves: Counties of Allegan, Ionia, Kent, Lake, Mason, Mecosta,
Montcalm, Newaygo, Osceola
www.aawm.org

Region 9 Northeast Michigan Community Services, Inc., Region 9 Area Agency on Aging
Phone: (989) 356-3474 or (800) 219-2273
Serves: Counties of Alcona, Arenac, Alpena, Cheboygan, Crawford, Iosco, Montmorency, Ogemaw, Oscoda, Otsego, Presque Isle, Roscommon
www.nemcsa.org

Region 10 Area Agency on Aging of Northwest Michigan
Phone: (231) 947-8920 or (800) 442-1713
Serves: Counties of Antrim, Benzie, Charlevoix, Emmet, Grand Traverse, Kalkaska, Leelanau, Manistee, Missaukee, Wexford
www.tcoa.org

Region 11 Area Agency on Aging
Phone: (906) 786-4701 or (800) 338-7227
Serves: Counties of Alger, Baraga, Chippewa, Delta, Dickinson, Gogebic, Houghton, Iron, Keweenaw, Luce, Mackinac, Marquette, Menominee, Ontonagon, Schoolcraft

Region 14 Area Agency on Aging
Phone: (231) 739-5858 or (800) 442-0054
Serves: Counties of Muskegon, Oceana, Ottawa
www.upcapservices.com
Association Office Area Agency on Aging Association of Michigan
6105 W. St. Joseph, Suite 209
Lansing, Michigan 48917
Phone: (517) 886-1029

APPENDIX B
Ombudsman Services in Michigan

Citizens for Better Care – Bridgeport
808 N. Michigan Ave.
Saginaw, MI 48602
Main: (989) 746-9216
Toll-Free: (866) 485-9393

Citizens for Better Care – Detroit
4750 Woodward Ave., Suite 410
Detroit, MI 48201
Main: (313) 832-6387
Toll-Free: (866) 485-9393

Citizens for Better Care – Grand Rapids
700 36th Street, SE, Suite 104
Grand Rapids, MI 49548
Main: (616) 245-9451
Toll-Free: (866) 485-9393

Citizens for Better Care – Lansing
P.O. Box 1219
Okemos, MI 48805
Main: (517) 347-7398
Toll-Free: (866) 485-9393

Citizens for Better Care – Traverse City
P.O. Box 5946
Traverse City, MI 49696
Main: (231) 947-2504
Toll-Free: (866) 485-9393

Kalamazoo Area Agency on Aging
Kalamazoo County Human Services Dept.
P.O. Box 42
Nazareth, MI 49074
Main: (269) 373-5157
Toll-Free: (866) 485-9393

Northeast Michigan Comm. Service Agency, Inc.
2375 Gordon Road
Alpena, MI 49707
Main: (989) 356-3474
Toll-Free: (800) 219-2273
Region 3-A Area Agency on Aging
P.O. Box 42
Nazareth, MI 49074
Main: (269) 373-5147

UPCAP Services, Inc.
2501 14th Avenue, South
Escanaba, MI 49829
Main: (906) 786-4701
Toll-Free: (800) 338-7227

APPENDIX C
Skilled Nursing Facility (SNF) Checklist*

Name of Skilled Nursing Facility: _____ Date of Visit:_____

	YES	NO	Comments
Basic Information			
The SNF is Medicare-certified.			
The SNF is Medicaid-certified.			
The SNF provides the skilled care you need, and a bed is available.			
The SNF has special services if needed in a separate unit (e.g. dementia, ventilator, or rehabilitation), and a bed is available.			
The SNF is located close enough for friends and family to visit.			
Resident Appearance			
Residents are clean, appropriately dressed for the season or time of day, and well groomed.			
Living Spaces			
The SNF is free from overwhelming unpleasant odors.			
The SNF appears clean and well kept.			
The temperature in the SNF is comfortable for residents.			
The SNF has good lighting.			
Noise levels in the dining room and other common areas are comfortable.			
Smoking is not allowed or may be restricted to certain areas of the SNF.			
Furnishings are sturdy, yet comfortable and attractive.			

	YES	NO	Comments
Staff			
The relationship between the staff and the residents appears to be warm, polite, and respectful.			
All staff wear name tags.			
Staff knock on the door before entering a resident's room and refer to residents by name.			
The SNF offers a training and continuing education program for all staff.			
The SNF does background checks on all staff.			
The guide on your tour knows the residents by name and is recognized by them.			
There is a full-time Registered Nurse (RN) in the SNF at all times other than the Administrator or Director of Nursing.			
The same team of nurses and Certified Nursing Assistants (CNAs) work with the same resident 4 to 5 days per week.			
CNAs work with a reasonable number of residents.			
CNAs are involved in care planning meetings.			
There is a licensed doctor on staff. Is he or she there daily? Can he or she be reached at all times? There is a full-time social worker on staff.			
The SNF's management team has worked together for at least one year.			

	YES	NO	Comments
Resident's Rooms			
Residents may have personal belongings and/or furniture in their rooms.			
Each resident has storage space (closest and drawers) in his or her room.			
Each resident has a window in his or her bedroom.			
Residents have access to a personal telephone and television.			
Residents have a choice of roommates.			
Water pitchers can be reached by resident.			
There are policies and procedures to protect residents' possessions.			
Hallways, Stairs, Lounges and Bathrooms			
Exits are clearly marked.			
There are quiet areas where residents can visit with friends and family.			
The SNF has smoke detectors and sprinklers.			
All common areas, resident rooms, and doorways are designed for wheelchair use.			
There are handrails in the hallways and grab bars in the bathrooms.			
Menus and Food			
Residents have a choice of food items at each meal (Ask if your favorite foods are served).			
Nutritious snacks are available upon request.			

	YES	NO	Comments
Staff help residents eat and drink at mealtimes if help is needed.			
Activities			
Residents, including those who are unable to leave their rooms, may choose to take part in a variety of activities.			
The SNF has outdoor areas for resident use and staff help residents go outside.			
The SNF has an active volunteer program.			
Safety and Care			
The SNF has an emergency evacuation plan and holds regular fire drills.			
Residents get preventive care, like a yearly flu shot, to help keep them healthy.			
Residents may still see their personal doctors.			
The SNF has an arrangement with a nearby hospital for emergencies.			
Care plan meetings are held at times that are convenient for residents and family members to attend whenever possible.			
The SNF has corrected all deficiencies (failure to meet one or more Federal or State requirements) on its last state inspection report.			

* Reproduced from Publication No. CMS-10153 Medicare Coverage of Skilled Nursing Facility Care, Department of Health and Human Resources, Center for Medicare and Medicaid Services

Notes

INDEX

A

Acceptance of Patient Advocate 15
Activities of daily living 23, 24, 26, 28, 29, 31, 34, 45, 107, 108
Adult day care 1, 24, 28, 31, 47, 48, 54, 56, 107, 114
Adult Foster Care (AFC) Homes 30
Adult foster care homes 30-31, 53, 64
Advance directives 11, 17, 37, 97
Age in place 23, 51, 54
Agent 12, 13, 14, 35, 52
Aging in place 27, 30, 97
Annuities 64, 82
Arizona 48, 95
Assessment 2, 26, 27, 29, 53
Asset Declaration form 63, 64, 65, 84
Assisted living 53, 99, 102, 107, 114, 115, 117
Assisted Living Federation of America 30
Authorized representative 84

B

Balloon annuity 82, 88
Basic Care 34
Benefit period 103

C

Care management 28, 29, 51, 52, 97
Care plan 27, 29
Caregiver agreement 78
Caregiver training 111
carryover basis 78
case management 53
cash assets 64
Cash benefits 102, 117
Center for Senior Independence 49
Chore services 47, 48
Chronically ill 108
Citizens for Better Care 9, 36, 52, 53, 124
Clear and convincing evidence 18
Colorado 48, 95
Community Health Accreditation Program 44
Community spouse 6, 62, 63, 65, 66, 69, 78, 80, 81, 83, 85, 86, 89, 91, 100

Community spouse resource allowance 63, 65, 85, 89, 91
Compound inflation 105, 106, 113
Conservator 17, 18, 19, 35
Continuing care retirement communities 24, 37, 57
Continuous period of institutionalization 64
Corporate Taxpayers 110
Custodial care 19, 28, 59

D
Department of Veterans Affairs 30
Divestment 5, 6, 62, 64, 70, 71, 72, 73, 77, 79, 80, 82, 83, 87, 88, 89
Do-Not-Resuscitate Orders 11, 17
Durable Medical Equipment 60, 111

E
Elimination period 102, 105, 107, 113, 114, 115, 117
Emergency Medical Response System 111
Estate plan 5, 14
Estate recovery 6, 94, 95
Evaluation 53

F
Family Care Benefits 102, 116
Fiduciary capacity 12
Form 2567 33

G
General durable power of attorney 11, 12, 13
General power of attorney for health care 11
Gerontology 53
Guaranteed Renewability 102
Guaranteed renewable 106
Guardian 12, 17, 18, 19, 84
Guardian ad litem 18

H
Health Care Financing Administration 33
Health insurance 4, 15, 16, 42, 59, 61, 69, 108, 109
HIPAA 16
HMOs 17
Home bound 17
Home care 1, 2, 3, 4, 5, 6, 7, 13, 27, 28, 29, 43, 47, 48, 49, 51, 52, 53, 54, 56, 81, 96
Home health agency 43

Home Help Program 41, 48
Home modifications 111
Home Safety Check 111
Homemaker 28, 47, 48, 52
Homes for the Aged (HFAs) 1, 29, 30, 31, 53, 64
Homestead 67, 68, 71
Hospital Discharge Planner 2, 44, 51, 53, 54
Household goods 67

I
Independent living 2, 24
Inflation Protection 102, 105
Institutional bias 4, 27, 32, 41-42, 48, 95-96
Institutional care 27, 48, 95
Instrumental activities of daily living 1, 26
Irrevocable funeral contract 67

J
Jewelry 67
Joint Commission of Accreditation of Heath-care Organizations 44
Jurisdiction 18

L
Letters of authority 19
living Wills 15
Long Term Care Task Force 55

M
Medicaid Home and Community Based Services Waiver
    for the elderly and disabled 47
Medicare Medicaid Assistance Program 43, 55
Medicare Part A 39, 43, 60
Medicare Part B 109
Medigap 56, 60, 61, 69
Medigap insurance 25
MI Choice 3, 45, 46, 47, 48, 52, 84, 94, 97
Michigan Department of Consumer and Industry Services 31
Michigan Hospice and Palliative Care Organization 39
Michigan Peer Review Organization 54
Minimum Data Set 26

N
National Adult Day Services Association 32
National Association of Home Care 44
National Hospice and Palliative Care Organization 39
Non-forfeiture 102, 115, 116
Non-legally responsible person 78
Nursing facility level of care criteria 45
Nursing home care 1, 4, 5, 6, 13, 23, 24, 29, 31, 34, 36, 37, 41, 42,
    44, 45, 46, 47, 49, 54, 60, 69, 77, 81, 94, 99, 100

O
Office of Financial and Insurance Services 38
Older Americans 28
Older Americans Act 41, 51
Ombudsman 2, 31, 33, 38, 51, 52, 53, 124
Oregon 48, 95

P
PACE 31, 32, 48, 49
Patient Advocate 14
Patient pay amount 68, 70
Personal care 28, 47
Personal liability 12
Petitioner 18
Policy limit 103, 104, 105, 115
Premium Chart: Guaranteed Renewable 112
Premium Differentials: Standard Class 114
Preponderance of the evidence 19
Presumed eligibility period 66
Principal 12
Principal residence 67, 68, 78
Private pay nursing homes 4
Probate court 3, 11, 12, 15, 18, 19, 20
Protective Order 20
Provider Care Check 111

R
Required minimum distribution 83
Respite care 28, 47, 48
Retirement communities 24, 56
Return of Premium Feature 102, 115
Risk retention 100

S

Self-deal 14
Self-employed taxpayers 110
Self-insurance 99, 100
Senior apartments 24, 25, 56
Shared care riders 102
Shelter allowance 69
Simple inflation 105, 106, 113
Single Point of Entry 55
Skilled care 34
Snapshot date 63, 64, 65, 66, 78, 81, 84, 91, 92
Social Security Administration 30, 60
Social work 53
Spousal allowance 66, 70
Spousal annuity trust 79, 80, 81, 82, 89, 92
State survey reports 33
stepped-up basis 78
Subsidized senior housing 25, 97
Substitute decision maker 12
Successor trustee 13, 14
Supplemental Security Income 20

T

Tax treatment 78, 102
Ten year averaging 83
Tenants in common 64
Testamentary special needs trust 86
The Michigan Aging Services System 48
The Patient Self Determination Act 17
Transportation 25, 43, 47, 48, 67, 78

V

Vermont 48, 95
Veterans Administration 42, 49

W

Waiting list 4, 35
Waiver agents 47
Waiver benefits 102, 116
Waiver of premium 102, 107
Waiver of premium benefit 102, 107
Waiver program 46, 47
Washington 48, 95

Notes

HOW TO CONTACT THE AUTHORS

P. Mark Accettura and Samuel A. Hurwitz are estate planning and elder law attorneys. Requests for information regarding Mark and Sam's legal practice, as well as inquires about their availability for speeches and seminars, should be directed to their address below. Readers of this book are also encouraged to contact Mark and Sam with comments and ideas for future editions.

P. Mark Accettura
Samuel A. Hurwitz
c/o Accettura & Hurwitz
35055 W. 12 Mile Road, Suite 132
Farmington Hills, MI 48331
248.848.9409 – phone
248.848.9349 – fax
Email: Mark (maccettura@agplc.com)
                 Sam (shurwitz@agplc.com)
Web site: www.agplc.com

ORDER COUPON

Send _____ copies of *Medicaid and Long Term Care in Michigan* at $12.95 per copy. Please add $3.95 postage and handling per book. Allow 7 days for delivery,

Send _____ copies of the *Michigan Estate Planning Guide* at $12.95 per copy. Please add $3.95 postage and handling per book. Allow 7 days for delivery,

Send _____ copies of *Lost and Found: Finding Self-Reliance After the Loss of a Spouse* at $19.95 per copy. Please add $3.95 postage and handling per book. Allow 7 days for delivery.

Name: _____

Company: _____

Address: _____

City/State/Zip: _____

Please make your checks payable to "Collinwood Press"
35055 W. 12 Mile Rd., Suite 132
Farmington Hills, Michigan 48331

QUANTITY DISCOUNTS AVAILABLE